I0605993

Ahem.

Giselle Clarkson

Omnibird

AN AVIAN INVESTIGATOR'S HANDBOOK

GECKO PRESS

CONTENTS

NOTES FROM 18 INVESTIGATIONS

HOW TO...

OMNIBIRDING AND YOU

Have you seen a bird today? Probably, unless you haven't got out of bed yet.

Doesn't mean I haven't seen YOU!

Ornithology = the study of birds

Avian = all things birdy

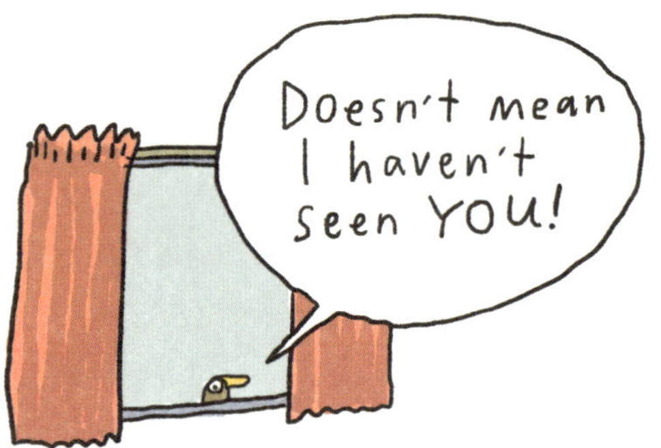

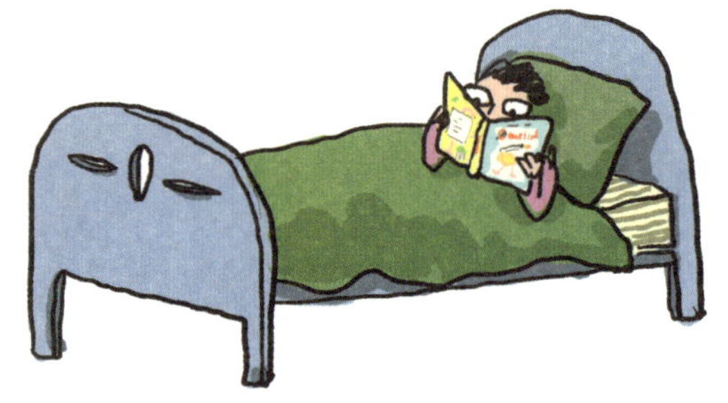

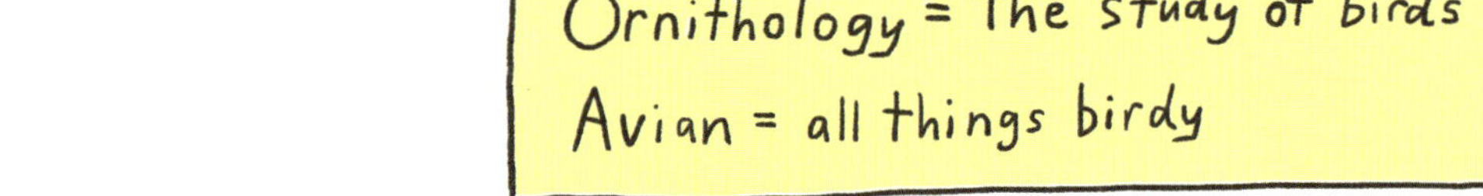

When we see something all the time, it's easy to forget that it's extraordinary. Mistaking the world for ordinary is a terrible habit that you should always struggle against. It's much worse than even picking your nose.

You can remind yourself how remarkable something is by breaking it up into pieces in your mind. A bird investigator specializes in doing this with birds.

Just look at this outrageous life form!

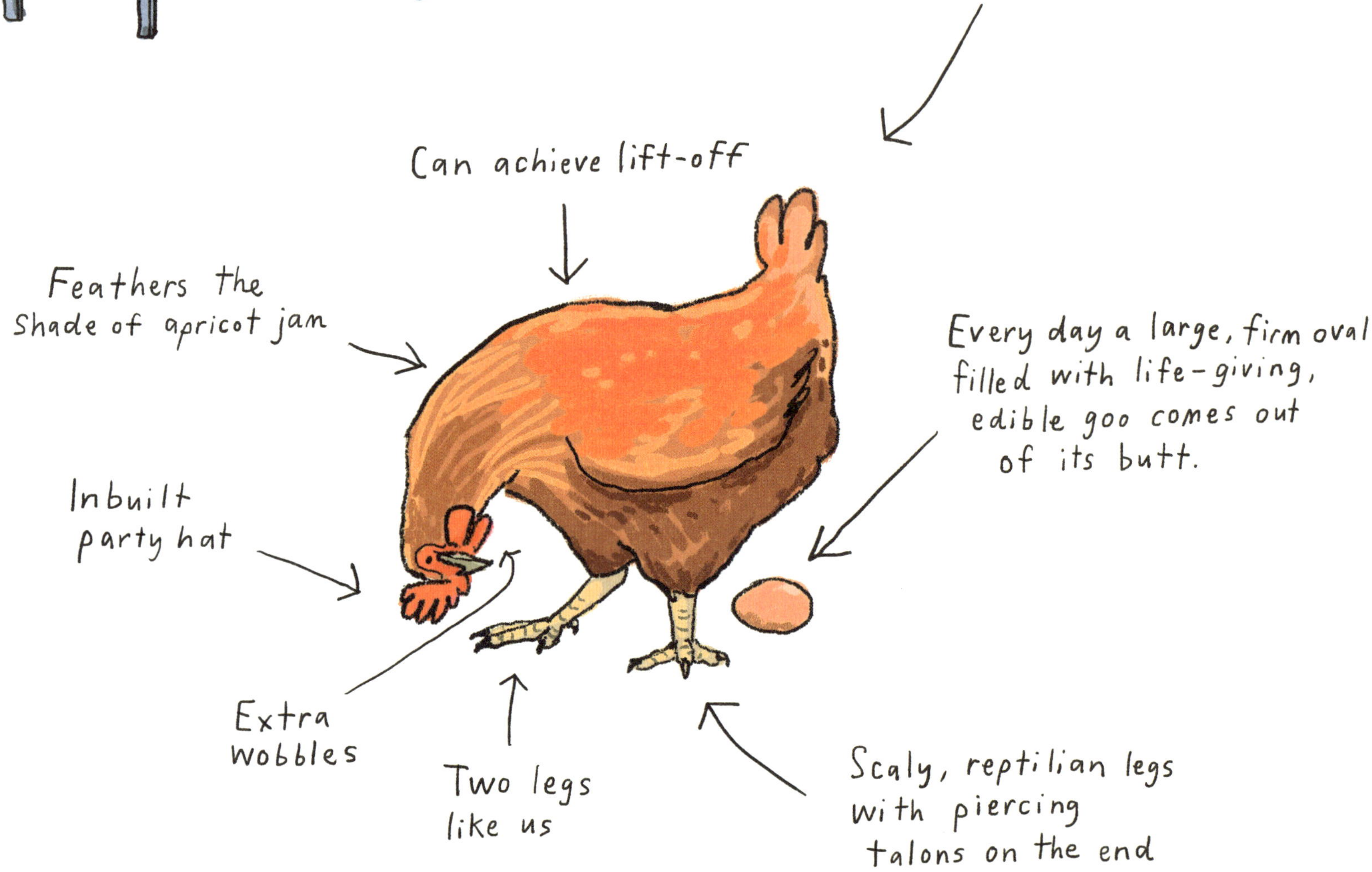

Can achieve lift-off
Feathers the shade of apricot jam
Every day a large, firm oval filled with life-giving, edible goo comes out of its butt.
Inbuilt party hat
Extra wobbles
Two legs like us
Scaly, reptilian legs with piercing talons on the end

EVERY DAY IS REPLETE WITH INVESTIGATIVE OPPORTUNITIES

Staring out the window

Participating in team sports

Eating lunch outside

Riding a bus

Focusing on the background of boring TV shows

Being dragged outside for some fresh air

Here's how an omnibirding investigator sees a flamingo.
Can't you make this page any taller?
Didn't brush its teeth this morning. Flamingos don't use toothbrushes. (They don't have teeth.)
It takes a lot of bones to make a neck this noodly. Flamingos have more bones here than a giraffe!
Just because it looks like it's made of strawberry ice cream, doesn't mean you should lick it.
A wide, scooping beak like this is shaped for sifting food out of water, not pecking fruit or sipping nectar.
It needs to keep its head on a pole so it can actually reach food down by its feet.
Strong, black feathers on its wing are a clue that it can probably fly.
Webbed feet mean it must live around water.
Legs and feet like this suggest you're not likely to see a flamingo in a tree or on a power line.
Long legs tell us it spends most of its time wading in shallow water.
This is an ankle, so in a way it's standing on its tippy-toes.
But these paddles will help it swim just fine whenever it takes the fancy.

Omnibird means "the universal bird," because when you're an avian detective you have a dossier of intelligence on every single bird in the universe (there are over 10,000 of them), even if you don't know their names.

Investigating a bird is like solving a puzzle. To gather all the pieces, you look for clues. What sort of beak does it have? What do its toes look like? Then you just need to learn which feet do which jobs and which beaks eat which meals (that's what this book is for), and you'll find you can deduce all sorts of facts about your bird and its way of life.

The more birds you inspect, the more you'll start to notice patterns, similarities and differences that will all add to your omnibird case file. You'll be able to look at any bird and see immediately which puzzle pieces fit.

Conveniently, you can investigate birds even when you can't see any. They leave clues everywhere.

In the same way a famous detective can tell what you had for breakfast by the pattern on your socks…

YOU can learn how to tell what a bird had for breakfast by the shape of its beak.

You can investigate a piece of fruit that's been pecked

Or a blob of poop on a park bench

DINOSAURS IN THE GARDEN

Thrillingly, the ancient ancestors of that sparrow outside your window were carnivorous dinosaurs called theropods.

When most dinosaurs went extinct, flighty little theropods survived because they were small, could travel by air and weren't fussy about what they ate.

Then evolution did its work for the next 65 million years and gave us all these magnificent creatures to live alongside us in our cities, streets, parks and backyards.

And what do you do with all this information when your brain is bulging with observations and knowledge? Some suggestions:

Impress your friends and family

Crime busting

Always have something to say to fill an awkward silence

Disaster management

So get out of bed (or just open the curtains), sally forth and detect avians wherever you go and at any time. Even daydreaming about what it would feel like to be a bird—that counts. Revel in the ludicrous and the beautiful, and remember, the world is very, very strange.

INVESTIGATIVE STRATEGIES

Some birds are much bolder than others. Sometimes it's because they've seen SO many people that they're not afraid, and in other cases it's because they've seen so few people, they don't know there's anything to be scared of.

In parks and towns, many birds will come close because you look like you could drop some food. Around wild birds, you need to employ more advanced techniques.

You could dress like a tree or a rock if it helps you get into character.

You can put birds at ease by acting as if you don't even care that they're there. If you stalk them like a predator, that's what they'll think you are.

Pretend you're not looking

Act like you're asleep

If you stumble across a dead bird, don't touch it as birds can carry disease that's harmful to humans. If you are careful, you can look at it or poke it (in a sensible way) with a stick. It might be the only time you ever see really close-up details, like whiskers and foot scales. If you have been near a dead bird, don't suck on your fingers or put them up your nose. That's dangerously foolish! Wash your hands thoroughly!

INVESTIGATING A BIRD THAT'S TOO FAR AWAY

When birds are way up in the sky, it can be tricky to see their usual distinctive features. It's hard to spot their beaks, and you can't usually see their feet at all, let alone count their toes. But a different set of clues reveals the identity of even the most distant bird.

Pigeon

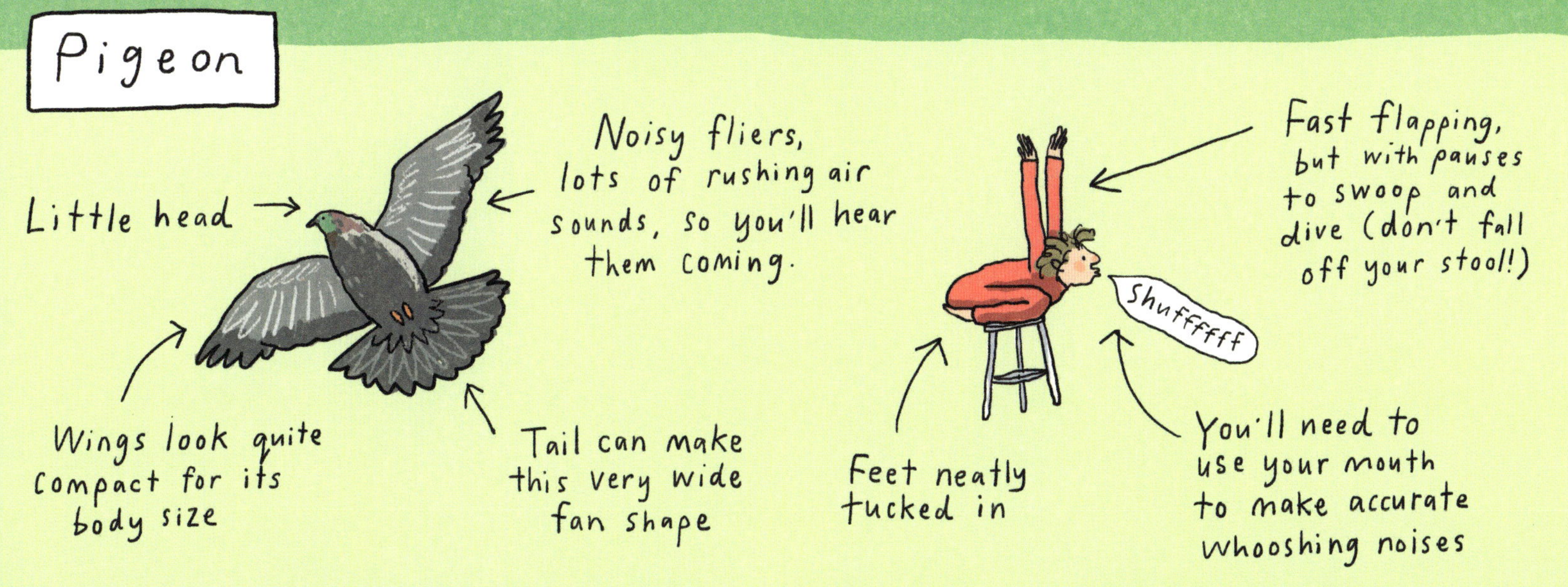

Little head
Noisy fliers, lots of rushing air sounds, so you'll hear them coming.
Wings look quite compact for its body size
Tail can make this very wide fan shape
Fast flapping, but with pauses to swoop and dive (don't fall off your stool!)
Shuffffff
Feet neatly tucked in
You'll need to use your mouth to make accurate whooshing noises

Parrot

Feathers separated at the tips
Blunt head shape
Trailing tail feathers (not this long on all parrots though)
Very broad wings
A consistant, steady, full-armed flap
SKARK!
Pretend your legs are your long tail

Finch

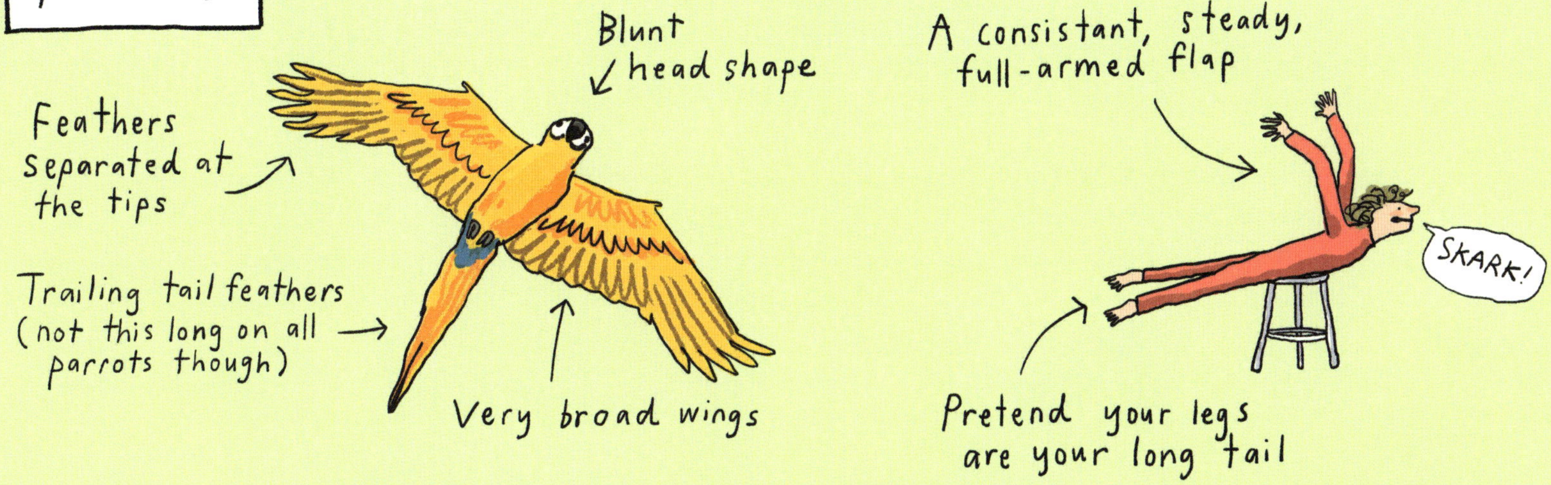

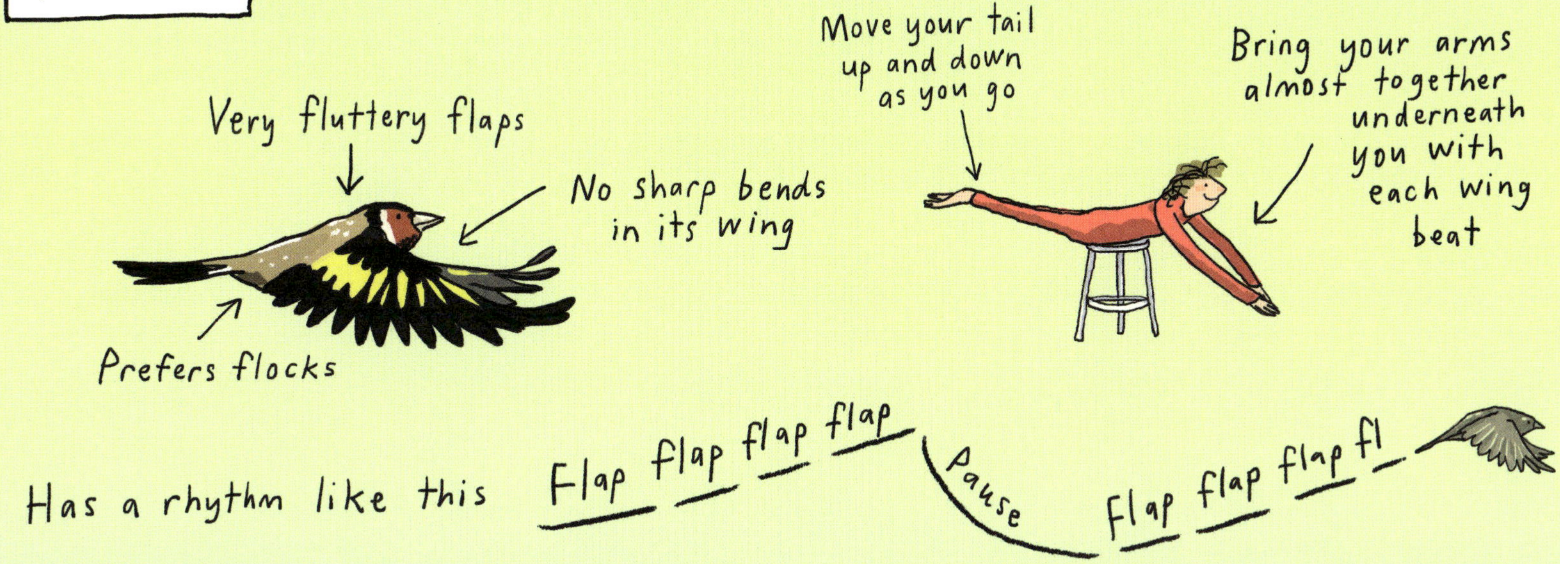

Very fluttery flaps
No sharp bends in its wing
Prefers flocks
Move your tail up and down as you go
Bring your arms almost together underneath you with each wing beat
Has a rhythm like this
Flap flap flap flap
Pause
Flap flap flap fl

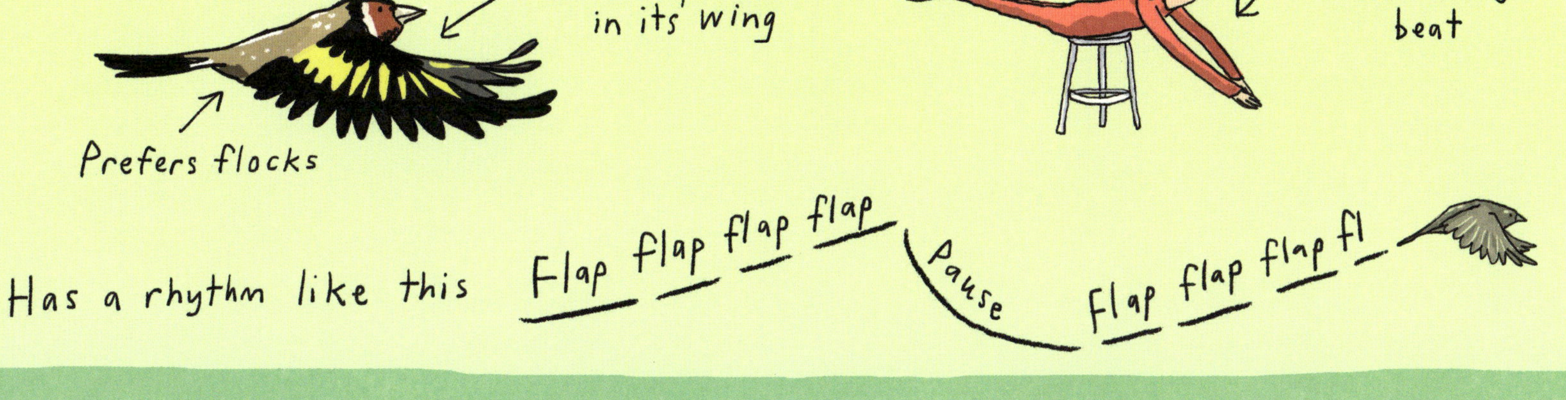

HIDE-AND-SEEK EXPERTS

When embarking upon an investigation, it's very important to be aware of all the anti-investigation tactics your subject will use. That way you'll know exactly where to look.

It's common for harmless insects to mimic poisonous ones, but very rare for birds. Adult cinereous mourners are grey-brown, but their chicks look like very big, hairy, toxic caterpillars. They even stick out their necks and squirm!

Dotterel chicks are like fluffy versions of the eggs they hatch from, speckled like beach pebbles.

Ptarmigans (the P is silent) change their outfits seasonally. In winter they're almost invisible against a snowy backdrop, and in summer they're dressed as lichen-covered rocks.

Bitterns are patterned just like the rushes they live among. They stand like this to blend in extra well.

Tawny frogmouths look more like tree branches than tree branches do sometimes. Until they open their eyes and mouth.

EAVESDROPPING

One of the nicest ways to conduct an investigation is to lie down in the sunshine, close your eyes and open your ears. Birds have a lot to say, so you might as well listen.

It's rare you'll ever find a bird that says something as mundane as tweet tweet. Birds croak, growl, roar, bellow, scream, warble, hoot, toot, hiss, boom, chuff, cackle, whistle and screech. Some birds barely say anything at all, but their wings go WHOOSH WHOOSH WHOOSH.

A good way to learn and remember different bird calls is to make up words or a rhythm that matches them.

WARBLING VIREO

If I sees you, I will seize you, I will squeeze you 'til you squirt!

UH-OH

Who cooks for you? Who cooks for you all?!

BARRED OWL

More pork. More pork.

RURU

YELLOWHAMMER

A little bit of bread and NO cheese!

Owl omelette!

LONG-TAILED DUCK

Potato chips!

AMERICAN GOLDFINCH

Not all owls say hoo-hoo. The famous hoot is from the great horned owl. Other owls opt for different noises.

Another way to remember bird calls is to draw them. When you're listening to a bird call, take a pen and draw a line. When the note is lower, the line goes down. When the note is higher, the line goes up. If the bird call is broken up into pieces, your line can do that too. Like this.

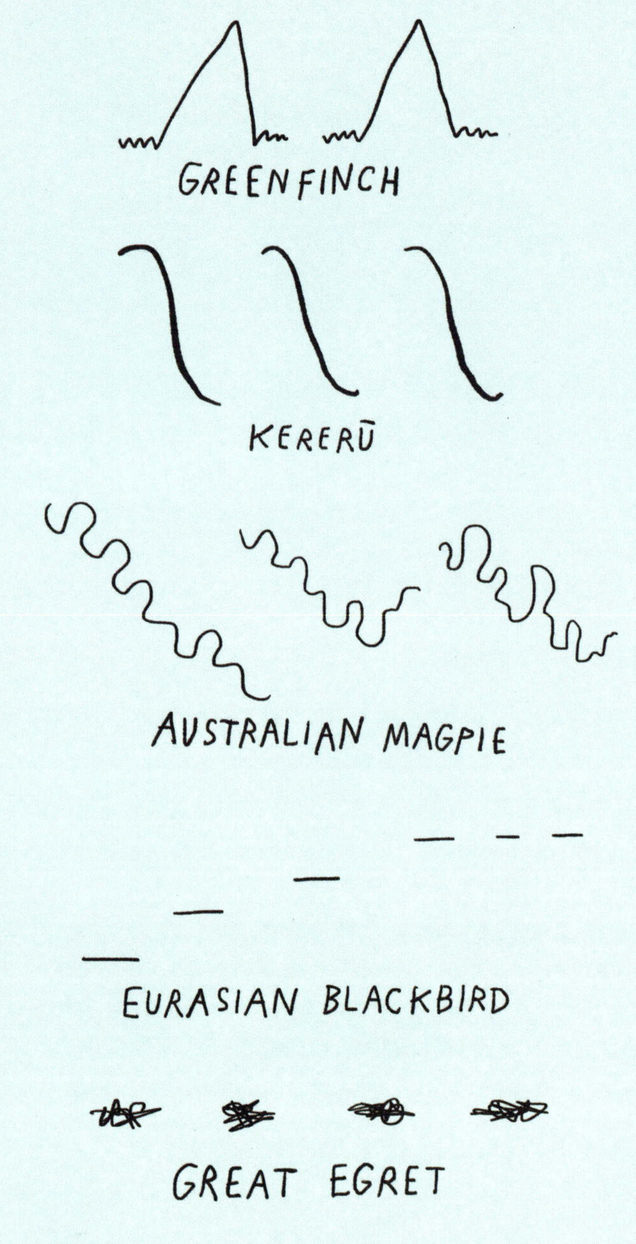

Perhaps no one else will know what it means. That doesn't matter—they can draw their own lines if they like. This is between you and the birds.

HOLDING A CONVERSATION

Sadly, without a bird's advanced voice box, and even with our excellent tongues and limber lips, we can't make all the same sounds that birds do. But that doesn't mean you shouldn't try.

1. You can whistle.

2. You can pinch your lips together extra tight and then breathe in to make really high-pitched squeaks.

3. Instead of saying, "Quack quack" to a duck, try to mimic its voice as closely as possible. Try saying, "Weh! Weh!" as if you want the words to come out of your nose.

Curious birds will wonder what on earth you're on about and come closer for a better look at you.

WHAT MAKES A BIRD A BIRD?

All birds are vertebrates, which means they have spines.

Animals without spines, like worms and beetles, are invertebrates.

All birds are warm-blooded. Fish and reptiles and amphibians have cold blood, but that doesn't mean they don't have warm and generous personalities.

All birds have beaks.

All birds lay eggs.

All birds have feathers.

ANATOMY OF AN OMNIBIRD (EXTERIOR VIEW)*

*SANS FEATHERS

Feathers, two legs and a beak are essential if you want to be a member of the bird club, but they can look like just about anything. Some bird species also have premium add-on features.

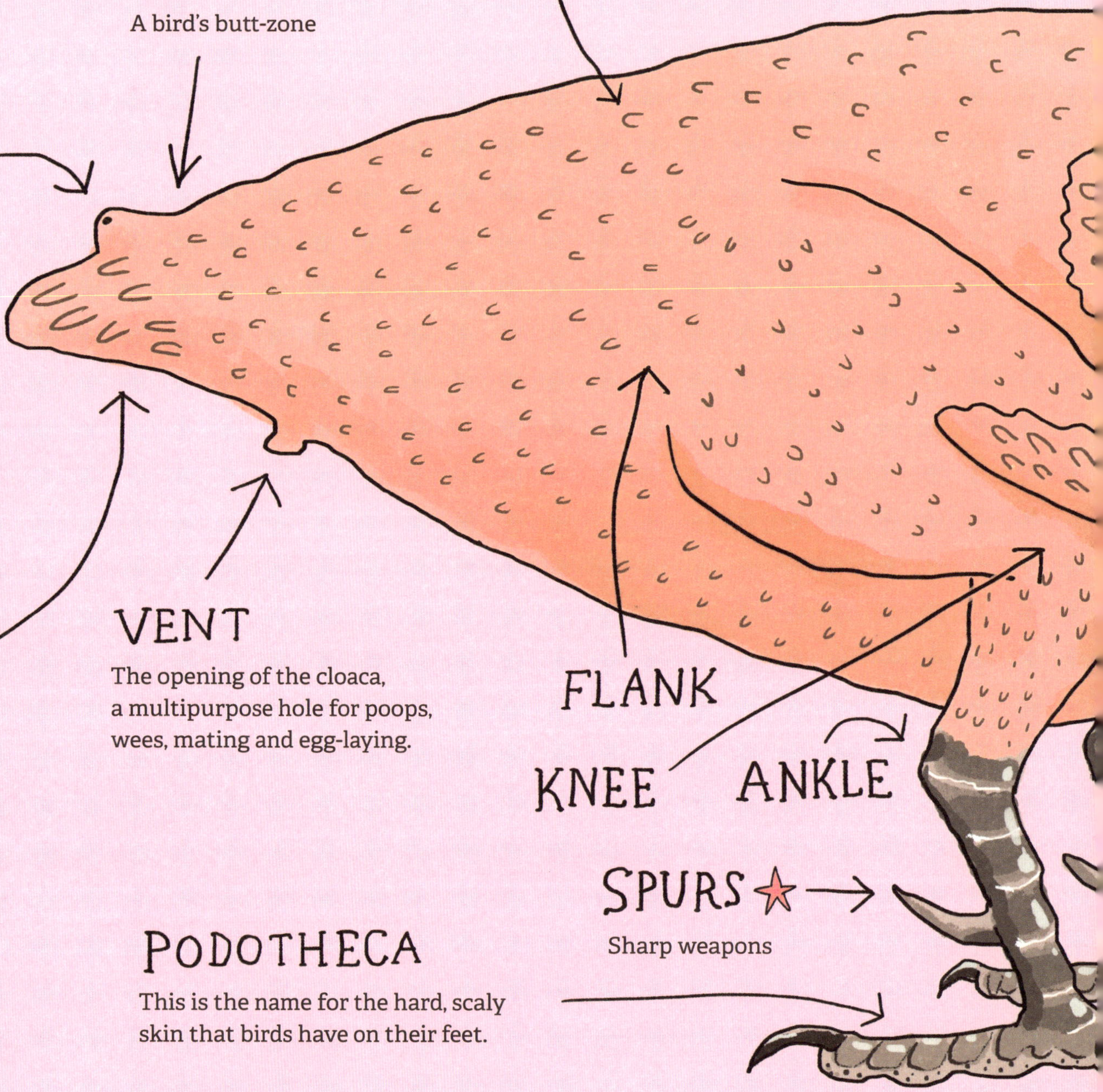

PTERYLAE

(ter-ih-lie)

The nubs on the skin where feathers sprout from. When you're cold enough to get goose bumps on your arms and legs, you look like this.

RUMP

A bird's butt-zone

PREEN GLAND ☆

A secret little nozzle that oozes feather-protecting oil. Birds with a preen gland use their beaks to spread the oil over all their feathers to keep them tidy, glossy and water-repellent. If you see a bird that keeps nibbling this spot on its back while performing its ablutions, it's probably a species with a preen gland.

TAIL

For balance and steering while flying, giving signals and showing off

VENT

The opening of the cloaca, a multipurpose hole for poops, wees, mating and egg-laying.

FLANK

KNEE

ANKLE

SPURS ☆

Sharp weapons

PODOTHECA

This is the name for the hard, scaly skin that birds have on their feet.

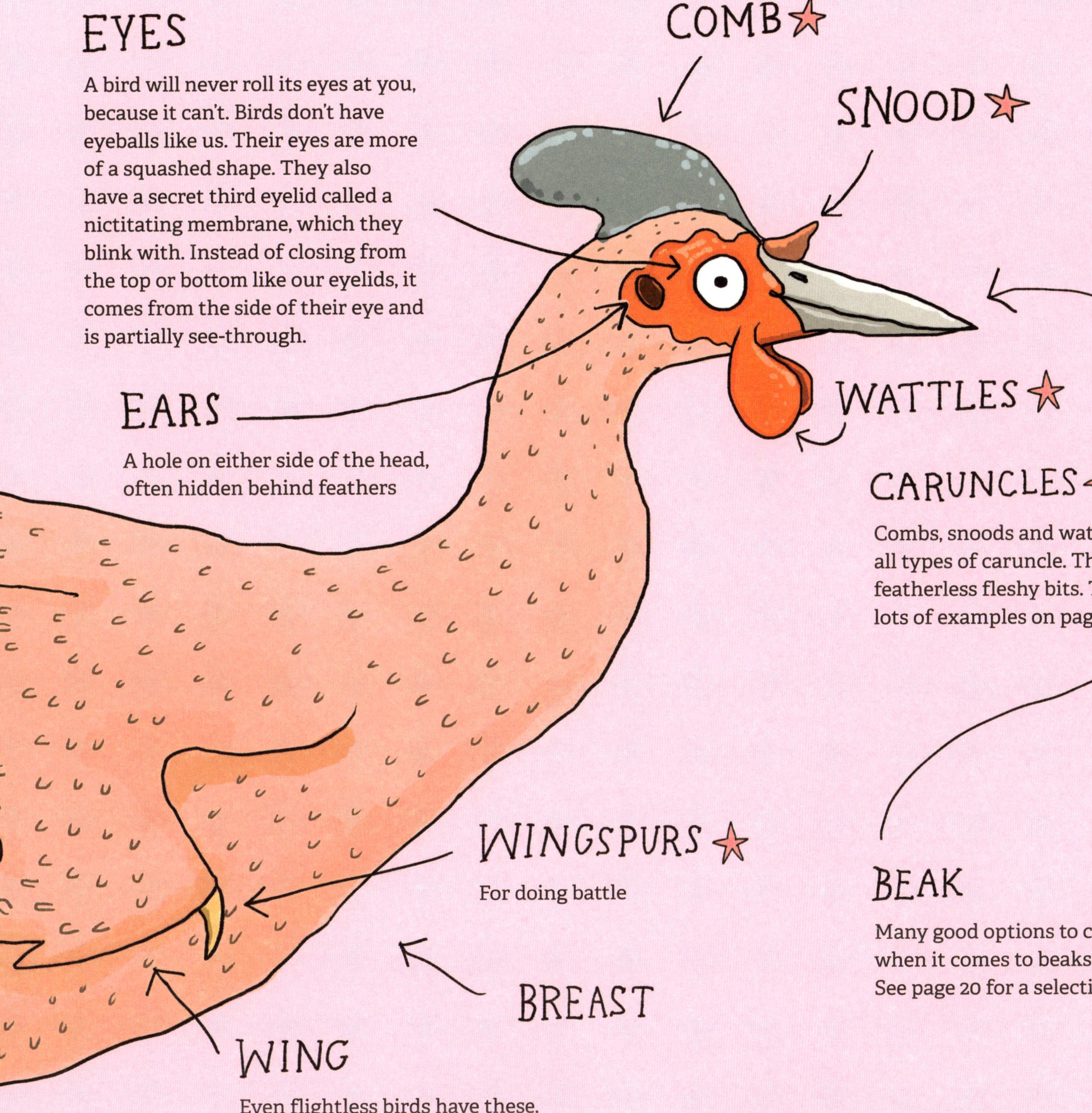

EYES

A bird will never roll its eyes at you, because it can't. Birds don't have eyeballs like us. Their eyes are more of a squashed shape. They also have a secret third eyelid called a nictitating membrane, which they blink with. Instead of closing from the top or bottom like our eyelids, it comes from the side of their eye and is partially see-through.

EARS

A hole on either side of the head, often hidden behind feathers

CARUNCLES ★

Combs, snoods and wattles are all types of caruncle. They are featherless fleshy bits. There are lots of examples on page 23.

WINGSPURS ★

For doing battle

BEAK

Many good options to choose from when it comes to beaks and bills. See page 20 for a selection.

BREAST

WING

Even flightless birds have these.

FEET

For a display of available options, see page 24.

LEGS

All birds start off with two. Sometimes one gets bitten off by a predator.

TALONS

Pointy toenails

★ Optional features

ANATOMY OF AN OMNIBIRD
(INTERIOR VIEW) (JUST THE HIGHLIGHTS)

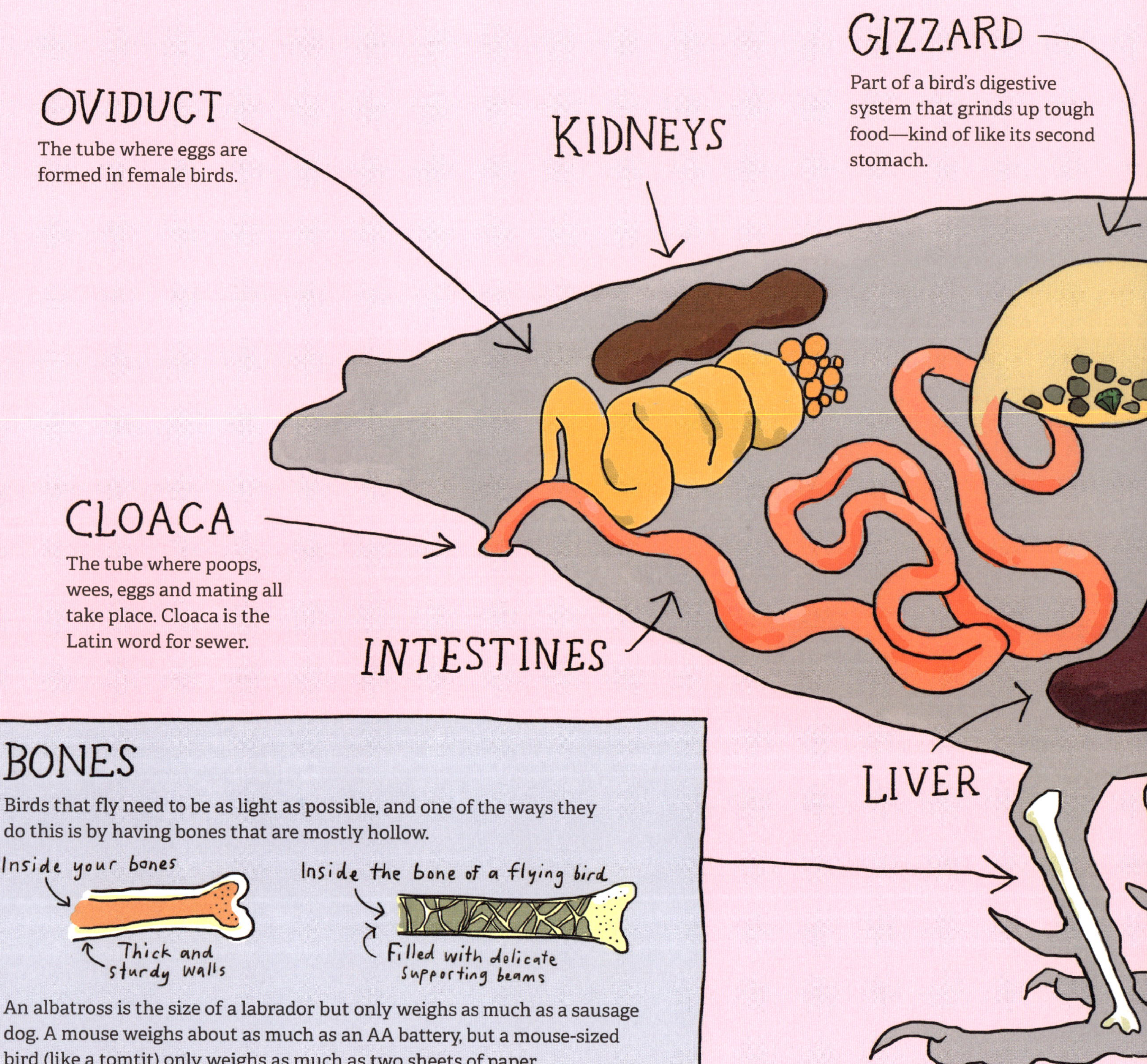

BONES

Birds that fly need to be as light as possible, and one of the ways they do this is by having bones that are mostly hollow.

An albatross is the size of a labrador but only weighs as much as a sausage dog. A mouse weighs about as much as an AA battery, but a mouse-sized bird (like a tomtit) only weighs as much as two sheets of paper.

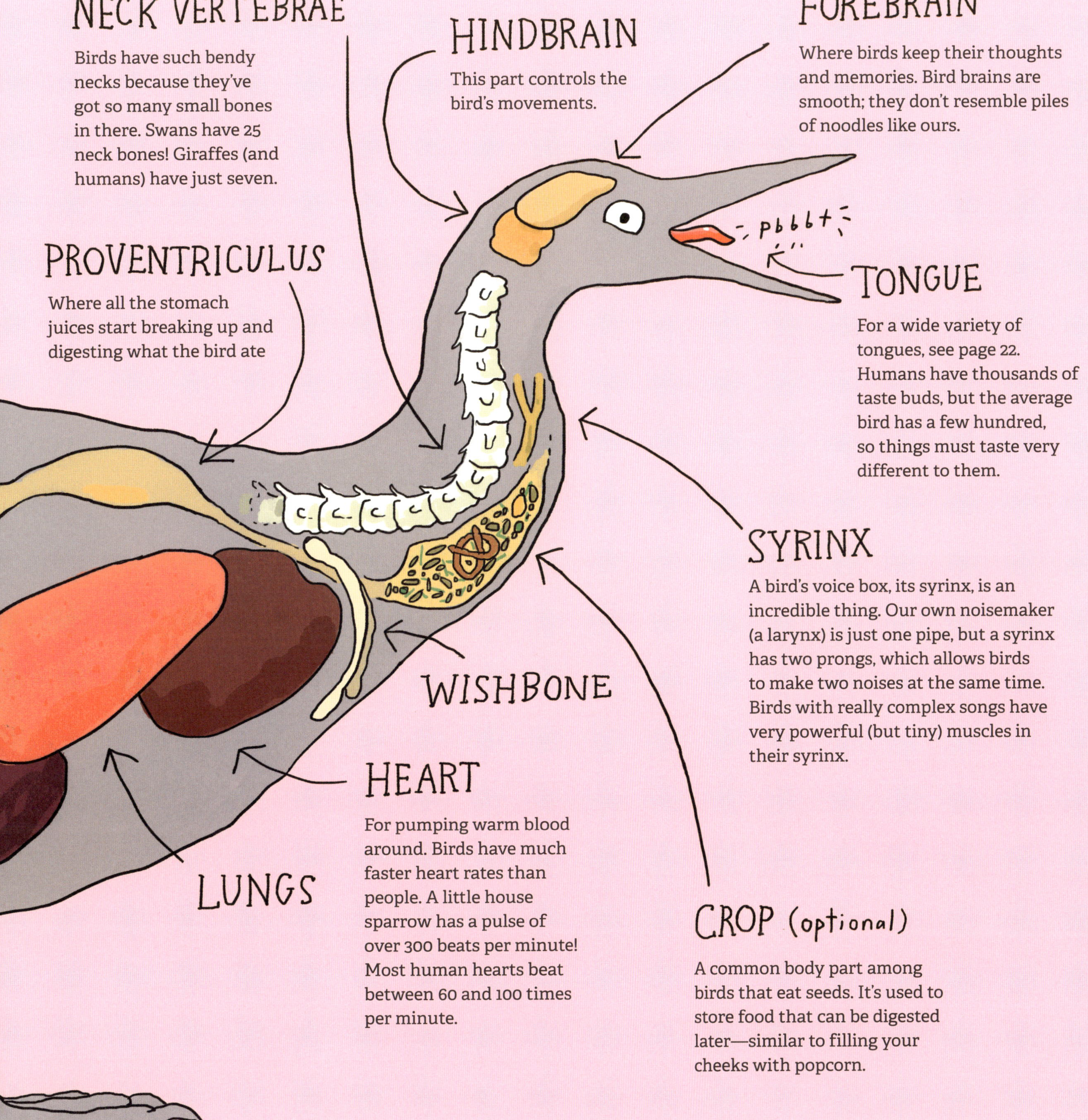
NECK VERTEBRAE
Birds have such bendy necks because they've got so many small bones in there. Swans have 25 neck bones! Giraffes (and humans) have just seven.
HINDBRAIN
This part controls the bird's movements.
FOREBRAIN
Where birds keep their thoughts and memories. Bird brains are smooth; they don't resemble piles of noodles like ours.
PROVENTRICULUS
Where all the stomach juices start breaking up and digesting what the bird ate
pbbbt
TONGUE
For a wide variety of tongues, see page 22. Humans have thousands of taste buds, but the average bird has a few hundred, so things must taste very different to them.
SYRINX
A bird's voice box, its syrinx, is an incredible thing. Our own noisemaker (a larynx) is just one pipe, but a syrinx has two prongs, which allows birds to make two noises at the same time. Birds with really complex songs have very powerful (but tiny) muscles in their syrinx.
WISHBONE
HEART
For pumping warm blood around. Birds have much faster heart rates than people. A little house sparrow has a pulse of over 300 beats per minute! Most human hearts beat between 60 and 100 times per minute.
LUNGS
CROP (optional)
A common body part among birds that eat seeds. It's used to store food that can be digested later—similar to filling your cheeks with popcorn.

BILLS AND BEAKS

What's the difference between a beak and a bill? Nothing! They're the same. Beaks are bills, and bills are beaks.

Scientists usually call them "bills." In everyday conversation, people tend to call pointy bills "beaks" and rounded beaks "bills."

The important thing is that the snappy parts of birds' mouths come in a prodigious array of shapes, with enough uses to fill a kitchen utensil drawer. Investigating a bird's beak can tell you a lot about how that bird lives and what it eats.

Beaks are mostly made of bone, so if you find an old skull, you can hypothesize what kind of bird it was from the shape of its beak bone.

The bone is covered in a layer of keratin, which is the same stuff our hair and fingernails are made out of. This outer layer can grow and change during a bird's life. Puffins even shed theirs and regrow it during mating season.

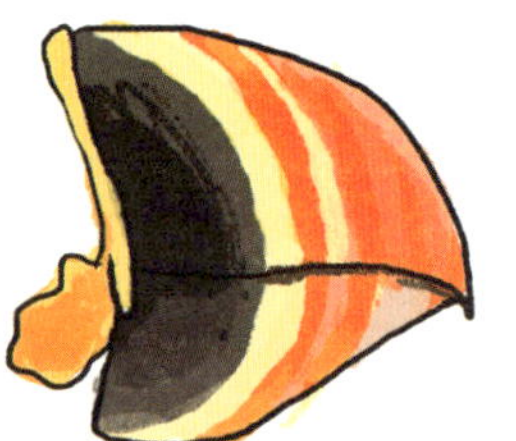

ATLANTIC PUFFIN DURING BREEDING SEASON

ATLANTIC PUFFIN THE REST OF THE TIME

MAXILLA (the top half)

NARE (bird nostril) You can sometimes see right through them.

TOMIA The sharp, cutty edges of a beak. They can have rough, almost toothy serrations.

TONGUE

LOWER MANDIBLE (the bottom half)

If birds had teeth like us they would be too heavy to fly.

SOME COMMON BEAK FORMS

HOOKED

A tool for ripping things apart—skin and muscle specifically, if you're a bird of prey. Also very helpful for climbing, if you're a parrot.

SHORT AND STURDY

Perfect for eating seeds. Sparrows and finches with beaks like this don't eat seeds whole. They crack them open and discard the husk, only eating the nutritious kernel inside.

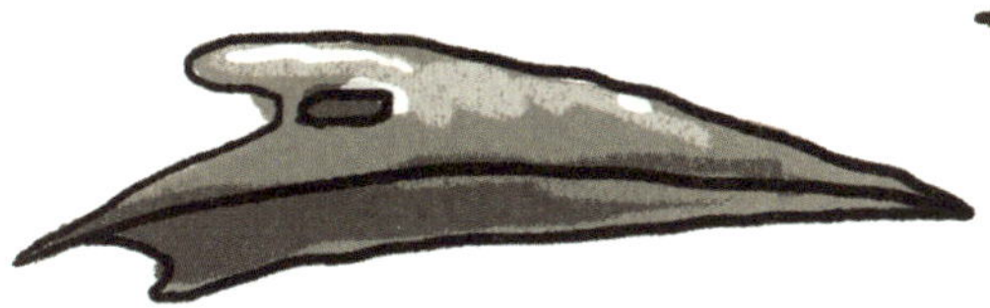

GENERALLY POINTY

This is a good beak for eating a bit of everything. It's a multipurpose tool for picking berries, pecking fruit, tearing leaves and snapping up juicy invertebrates.

VERY LONG AND SKINNY

A spear like this is for poking into soft mud and plucking out frogs and crabs, and catching fish.

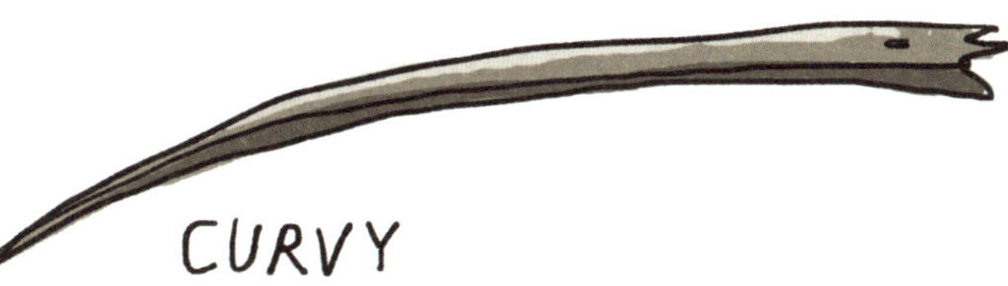

CURVY

This one's for poking into hard to reach spots, like the bottom of a really long flower. Birds that mostly drink nectar have beaks like this.

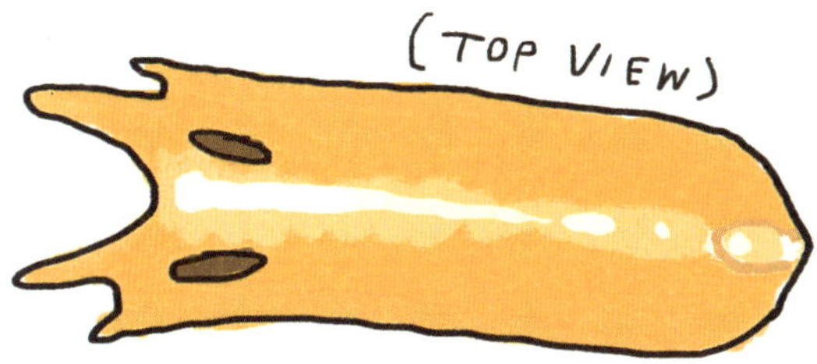

WIDE AND FLAT

Ideal for foraging in water because it can be used to filter out all the liquid from the solids.

SOME ODDITIES

BLACK SKIMMER

Their lower mandible is a scoop. They skim it through the water until it touches a fish. And then, SNAP!

WRYBILL

A beak that curves to the right for reaching mayfly larvae underneath rocks.

CROSSBILL

A lever that's just right for prising apart conifer cones and getting the seeds out.

TONGUES

Your tongue is shaped like it is for helping you chew and swallow sandwiches and ice creams and curries, and lick your plate afterwards. Birds have entirely different tongues because they eat moths, fish, berries or nectar, and they don't use plates. Here are some particularly interesting models.

LORIKEET

A sturdy tongue with a dainty little brush at the tip is perfect for coaxing pollen and nectar out of flowers. And tickling your ear, probably.

WOODPECKER

Not only are woodpecker tongues exceedingly long, perfect for probing around inside insect burrows, they're also covered in gluey spit. Insects get stuck like they would on a bit of flypaper.

HUMMINGBIRD

Snakes and lizards aren't the only animals with forked tongues—hummingbirds have them too. Nectar gets trapped in fine hairs between the forks, making it easier to slurp.

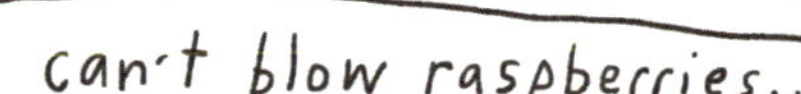

KINGFISHER

Long beaks don't always hold long tongues. Kingfishers have teeny weeny tongues, which help to direct squirming frogs and fish down their throats.

PENGUIN

Just as fish hooks have a backwards barb to stop fish from wriggling free, penguin tongues are completely covered in bristly spines, making their whole mouth a one-way system for even the slipperiest meal.

TOUCAN

Toucan tongues seem like an odd match for their enormous bright bills. They look like a very long, thin feather and help to grip and manage their food (which is mostly fruit but can include insects, little lizards and other birds' eggs).

CARUNCLES

Caruncles are mostly there to make birds look dashingly handsome, and I think you'll agree that they do the job well. Big, bright caruncles signal to other birds that the bearer is in excellent health and ready to breed. Chicks don't have caruncles; they only develop with age. Caruncles grow in a lot of exciting forms. If you touch them they're warm and silky soft.

A lot of birds just have one or two types of caruncle; others are thrillingly caruncle-rich.

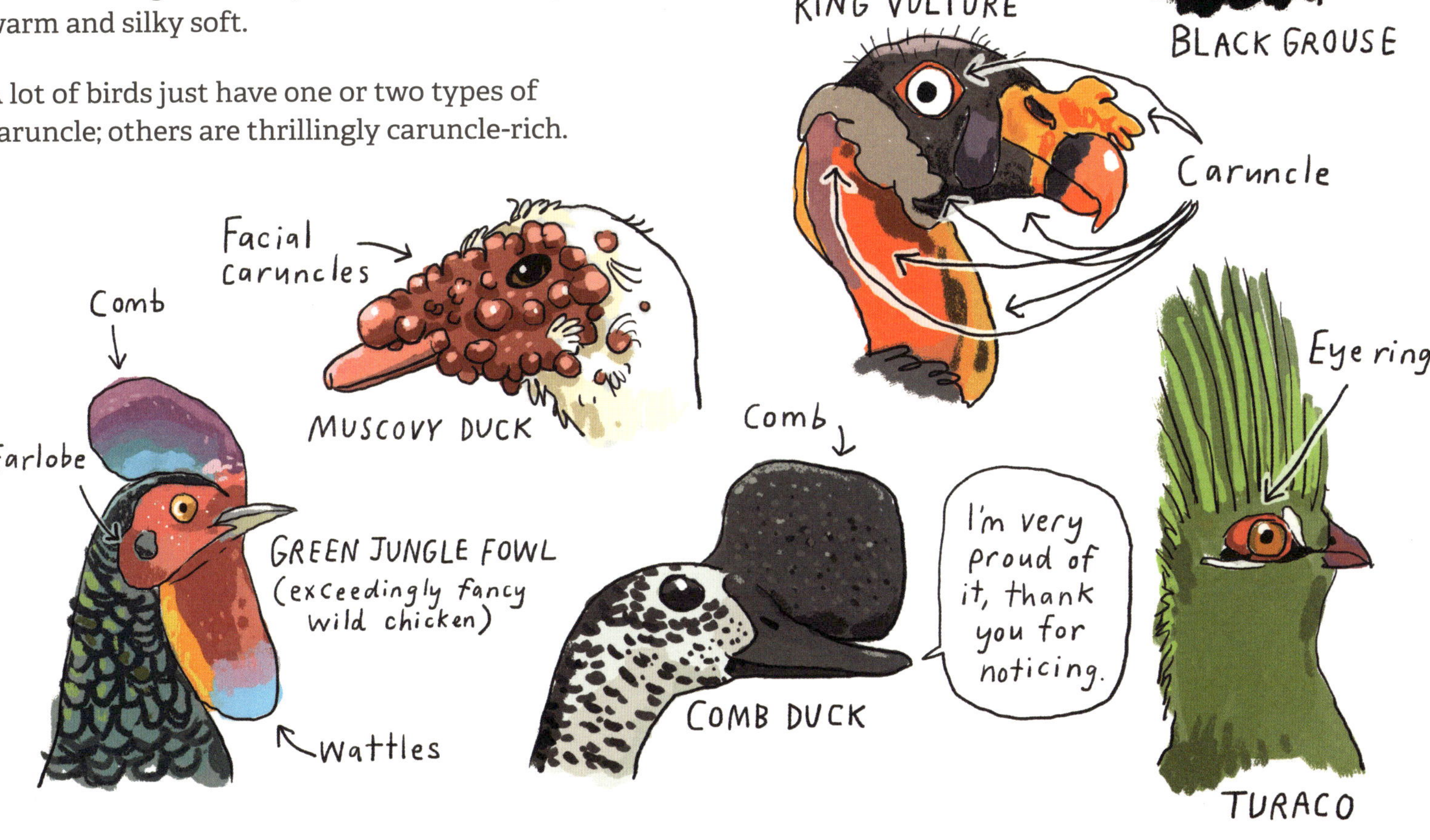

SNOOD MOODS

Male turkeys are majorly caruncled. They've got almost no feathers at all on their heads and necks.

When they want to show off, they pump extra blood into their heads, which makes their skin flush in magnificent shades of red and blue and transforms their snood from a little nub into a big, dangly worm.

FEET

Like you, all birds have hard bits on the end of each toe. They keep theirs sharp for gripping branches or food, or for fighting with. You have to keep yours blunt or else you'd ruin all your socks.

A thorough investigation of an avian foot will reveal many clues about the owner's lifestyle. Every tootsie has a purpose, identifiable by its size and shape.

Long skinny toes aren't the best for paddling, and webbed feet aren't particularly good for clinging on to spindly branches. Some birds defy expectations though, so watch out for astonishing rule breakers!

ACCEPT NO LIMITATIONS, COMRADES!

Some flappy footed Shags roost and nest in twiggy trees.

Weka have feet like chickens but are excellent swimmers.

HEAR HEAR!

FOOTPRINTS

When you know whose toes are whose, you can look at any avian footprint and make an educated deduction about what kind of bird has been stomping around before you arrived on the scene.

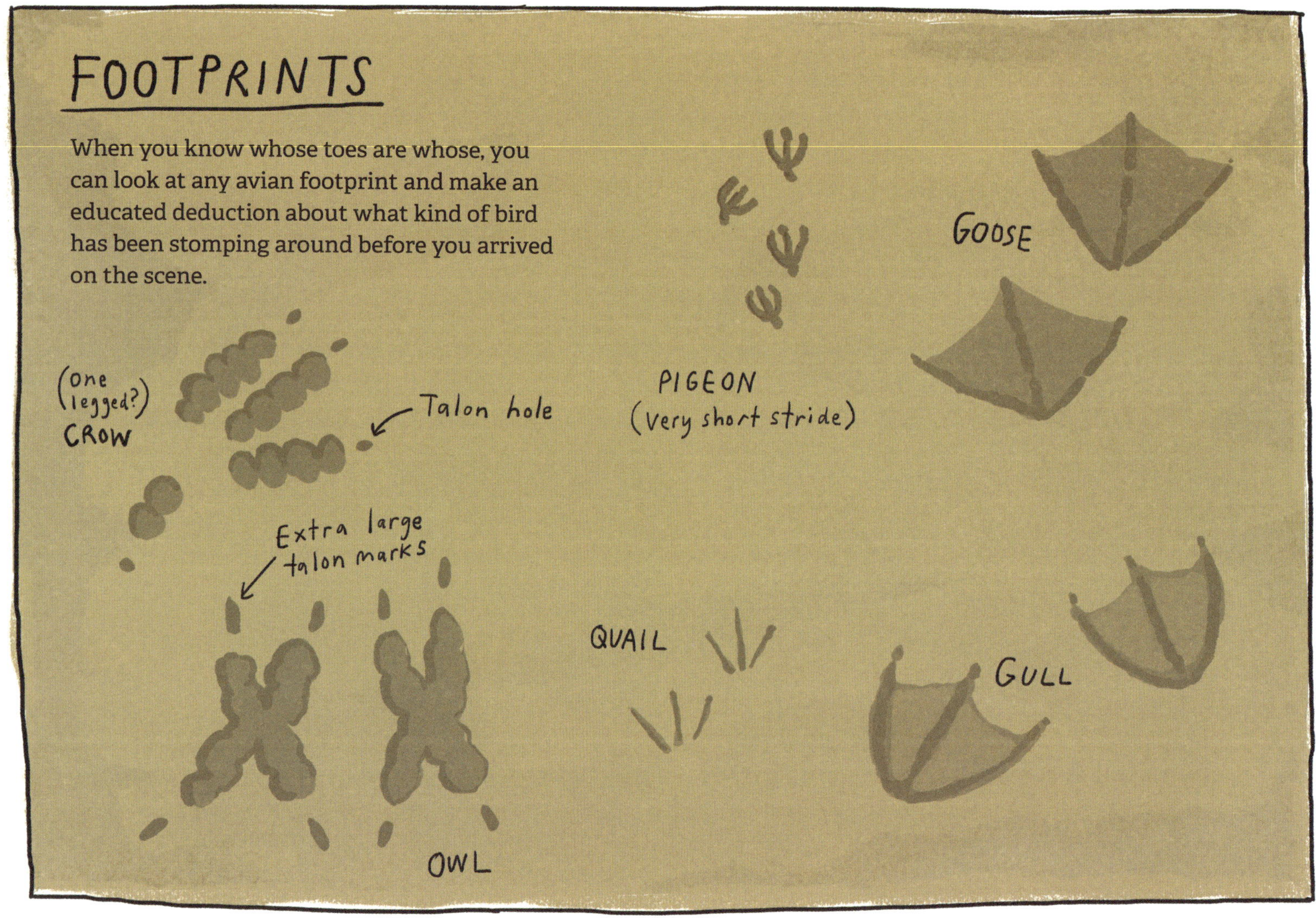

Most birds have four toes, but the direction they sprout in depends on what the bird intends to use them for.

THE ALL-AROUNDER (Anisodactyl)

This is an excellent multipurpose foot. It's great for walking and hopping and perching, so it's the most common type of bird foot out there.

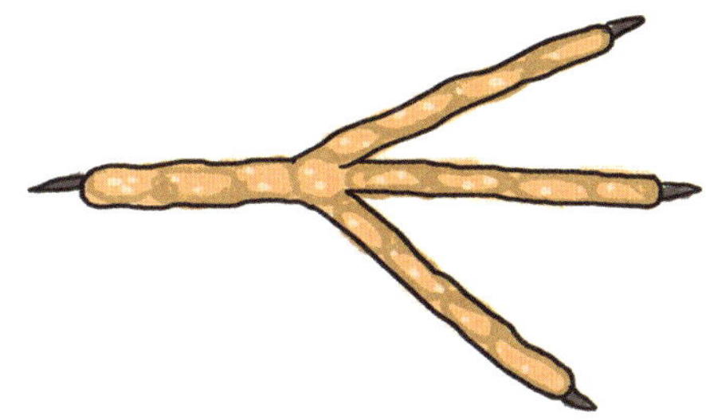

EXTRA GRIPPY GRAPPLE (Zygodactyl)

This is the kind of foot parrots have. Two toes face forward and two toes face back, and they can clutch onto things in a way not outrageously different from us with our thumbs.

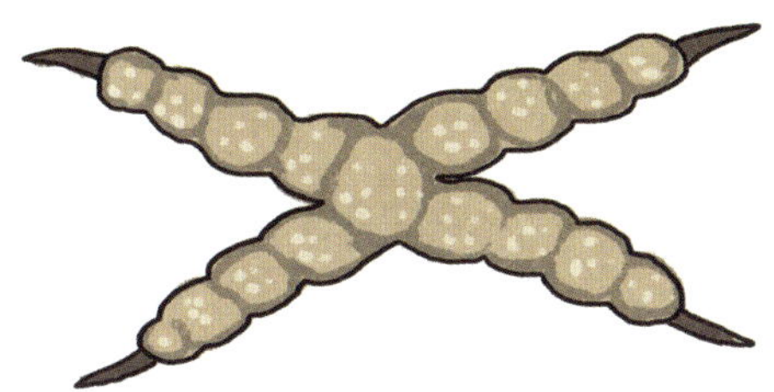

PADDLES (Palmate)

Palmate feet have three toes webbed together to use as paddles. They make a wonderful slapping sound when they walk across a smooth surface.

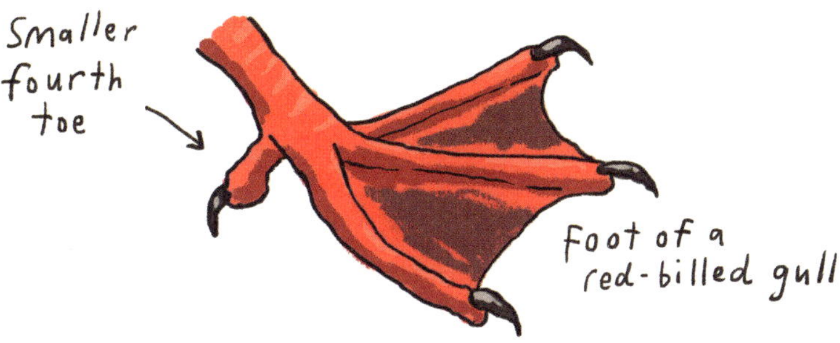

PADDLES PLUS (Totipalmate)

Totipalmate feet have FOUR toes webbed together for even better paddles, and even better slapping.

BLOBBY (Lobate)

Coots have some of the most wonderfully strange feet of any bird. They're a water bird, but instead of webbing they have a whole lot of lobes.

ANTI-SINKING TOES

Either webbed feet or extra long skinny toes on the end of very long legs are good for birds that wade around in boggy places. Having very wide feet stops them from sinking in, like when people wear snow shoes.

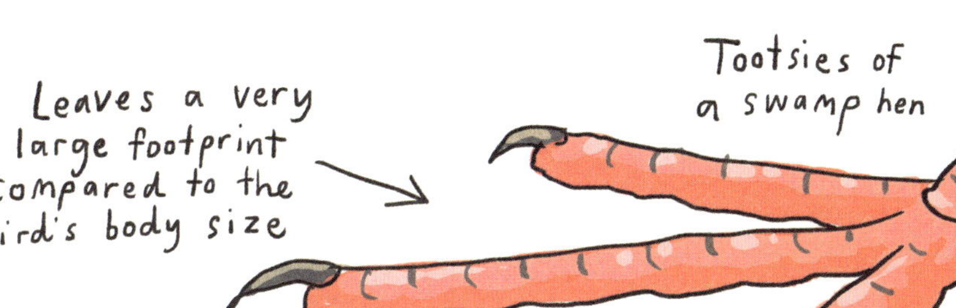

PLUMOLOGY (the study of feathers)

Just like our hair can be straight, curly, bristly or fine depending on where it sprouts from, so can a bird's feathers. When you find a loose feather on the ground, inspect it closely and you'll be able to tell what the bird used it for.

THE SEVEN MAIN TYPES OF FEATHER

WING

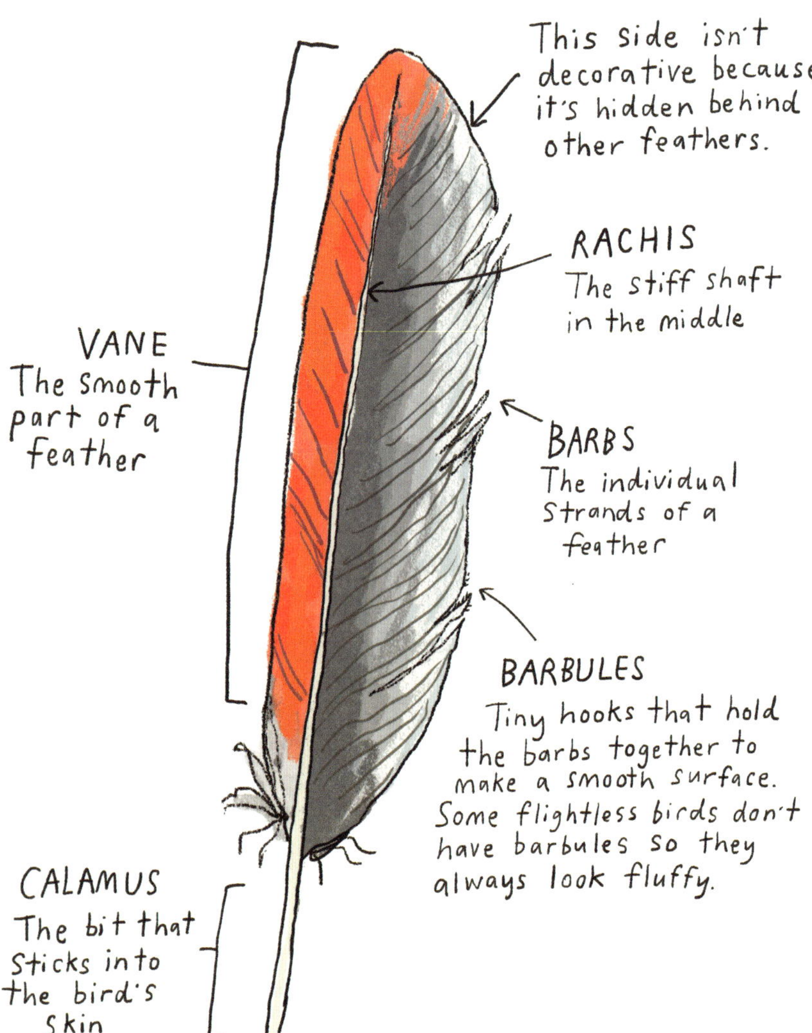

Stiff, asymmetrical feathers on a bird's wing, shaped perfectly for balance and strength while flying.

TAIL

Strong and sturdy, tail feathers are similar to wing feathers but more symmetrical. Good for balance and steering while in the air.

CONTOUR

These feathers cover most of a bird's body, layered neatly like fish scales to make a flexible, waterproof coat.

DOWN

The softest feathers with no rachis and no hooks to hold the barbs together. Down grows right next to the bird's skin and traps heat to keep birds cozy. You might find down feathers leaking out of your pillow or winter coat.

SEMIPLUME

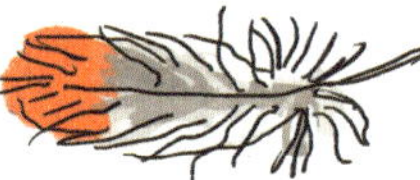

Half contour, half down... mostly there for warmth, and found all over the bird's body.

FILOPLUME

These delicate tufts are very small and close to the skin. It's possible that birds use them as a sense to tell them when their other feathers need preening, or to measure air or water flow when they're flying or swimming.

BRISTLE

Usually found around a bird's face like whiskers, bristles protect the bird's eyes from bugs and dirt.

FEATHERED AREAS OFTEN USED IN BIRD NAMES

Common names for birds often refer to an area of their feathers. It makes the birds easier to identify if you know which bit they're talking about.

AVIAN ATTIRE

When males and females of a species look different from one another, it's called sexual dimorphism.

Different sexes of birds like gulls and penguins look alike, and it can be hard even for scientists to tell who's who. A lot of the time, the only way to know for sure is by taking a blood sample and processing it in a laboratory. Other birds are so sexually dimorphic you might not even think the male and female are the same species!

When males are so dramatically decorated, it's easy to overlook the quieter beauty of the females.

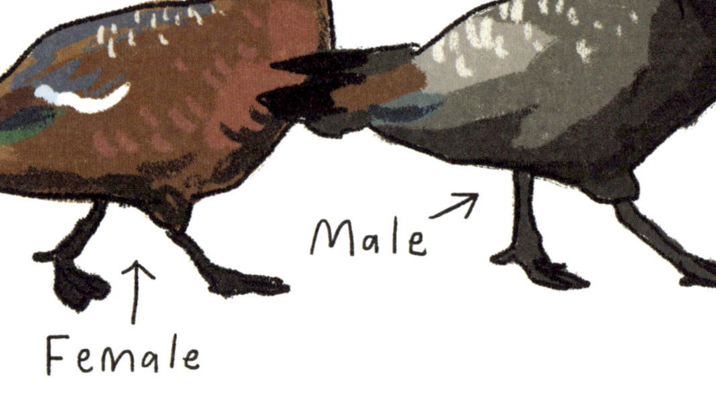

Just to really complicate things, male birds don't always wear their fanciest outfits. Outside of breeding season (when they're trying to attract attention), their feathers can be duller and more like a female's.

Every now and then, a bird hatches with one of these conditions, making them stand out from the rest of their species.

SNOWY WHITE (Albinism)

A bird with albinism has no melanin. Melanin is what makes skin and feathers darker. An albino bird will have completely white feathers and pink eyes. They often look scruffy because melanin also makes feathers strong—that's why birds that fly often have black wing-tips. Sadly, albino birds don't live long in the wild. They have poor eyesight and no camouflage, making them sitting ducks for predators (even if they're not ducks).

EXTRA DARK (Melanism)

A melanistic bird has extra melanin. Its feathers are darker than usual or even black.

VERY PALE (Leucism)

A leucistic bird has *some* melanin. It will look like a white, muted or blond version of its species. These birds have dark eyes.

It's possible for a bird to be partially leucistic.

HALF AND HALF (gynandromorphism)

Very, very, extremely occasionally, a bird will be exactly half female and half male. They are absolutely remarkable, and you'd be the envy of a lot of people if you saw one. In species where males and females look quite alike, they might not be so easy to spot. But it's really spectacular on this northern cardinal.

EGGS

A bird's egg must be one of the most fantastic, almost magical things to exist on earth. It is as beautiful and smooth as a precious stone, and when you apply heat, a new life grows inside it. Extraordinary.

Laying eggs is a really important part of being able to fly. If birds had to carry around a growing baby like a mammal does, they'd gradually get heavier and heavier until they couldn't take off anymore.

OOLOGY

Before people got wise and figured out that pinching pretty eggs straight from the nest of wild birds was not a good thing to do (and made it illegal), it was a popular hobby called oology—a great word because all the o's look like eggs. But at least all those stolen eggs aren't going to waste; they're kept in museums where scientists can study them.

Two substances make up the rainbow of birds' eggs: one is greeny-blue and the other is reddish-brown. Just like paints, mixing different amounts of each gives different results.

As a general rule—remember that there are always exceptions—birds that lay their eggs out in the open have patterned, camouflaged eggs so predators won't spot them. Eggs that are laid in burrows or holes in trees are already hidden, so they're plain white.

AN EGG'S JOURNEY TO THE NEST

A female bird assembles eggs inside her like a production line in a factory. It's like taking a nut, dipping it in jam, wrapping it in marzipan and then coating it in chocolate (with optional nuts or sprinkles for decoration).

OVARY

Here is the beginning of every egg the bird will lay in her lifetime, waiting for its turn.

YOLK

The yolk is food for the growing chick. (This one is next in line to be laid.)

INFUNDIBULUM

Where the sperm meets the egg and fertilizes it. If there's no sperm, the yolk just carries on down the line but won't ever turn into a chick.

MAGNUM

Here, the yolk gets its first layers of albumen (egg white). Albumen keeps the chick cushioned while it grows..

UTERUS

The shell is made, and any decorations are added right at the end.

ISTHMUS

The developing egg gets membranes and more layers of albumen.

DOUBLE-YOLKERS

Sometimes two yolks slip out of a hen's ovary at once and get bundled up together in the same egg. This is most likely to happen if a chicken has just started to lay eggs for the first time, or if her egg-laying days are nearly over.

If the yolks are fertile, it IS possible for them to hatch as twin chicks, but it's very rare for both to survive.

LOVELY OVAL OVA!

"Ovum" is the scientific word for "egg," and the plural is "ova." It comes from Latin and is the same place we get the word "oval" from.

SOME OF THE EXTRAORDINARY EGGS THAT YOU'RE MOST LIKELY TO MEET

DISSECT YOUR BREAKFAST

A chicken egg plucked from a carton is as wondrous as any wild bird's egg, and finding one is elementary for even an amateur sleuth. This makes them perfect to marvel at, and allows you to observe things that are true for ALL eggs, even the very rare and brightly decorated ones.

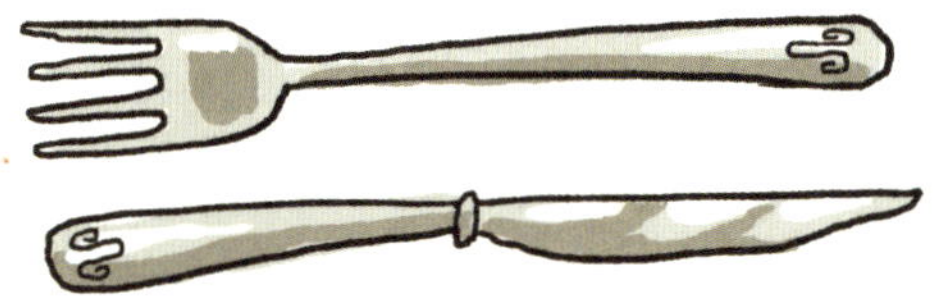

DISSECTING EQUIPMENT

Not all eggs look like this when you boil them. African penguin eggs stay completely clear like jelly when they're boiled.

We'll probably never know what some eggs look like when they're cooked. The world is full of wonderful mysteries.

If you peel a boiled egg you'll see the dip where the air pocket was.

Eggs are laid with an air pocket that gradually grows larger over time. That's why older eggs float to the surface in a pot of water, because they've got more air inside. It doesn't always mean they're rotten.

This very delicate filmy layer is the membrane.

SHELL
It's riddled with tiny pores, like our skin.

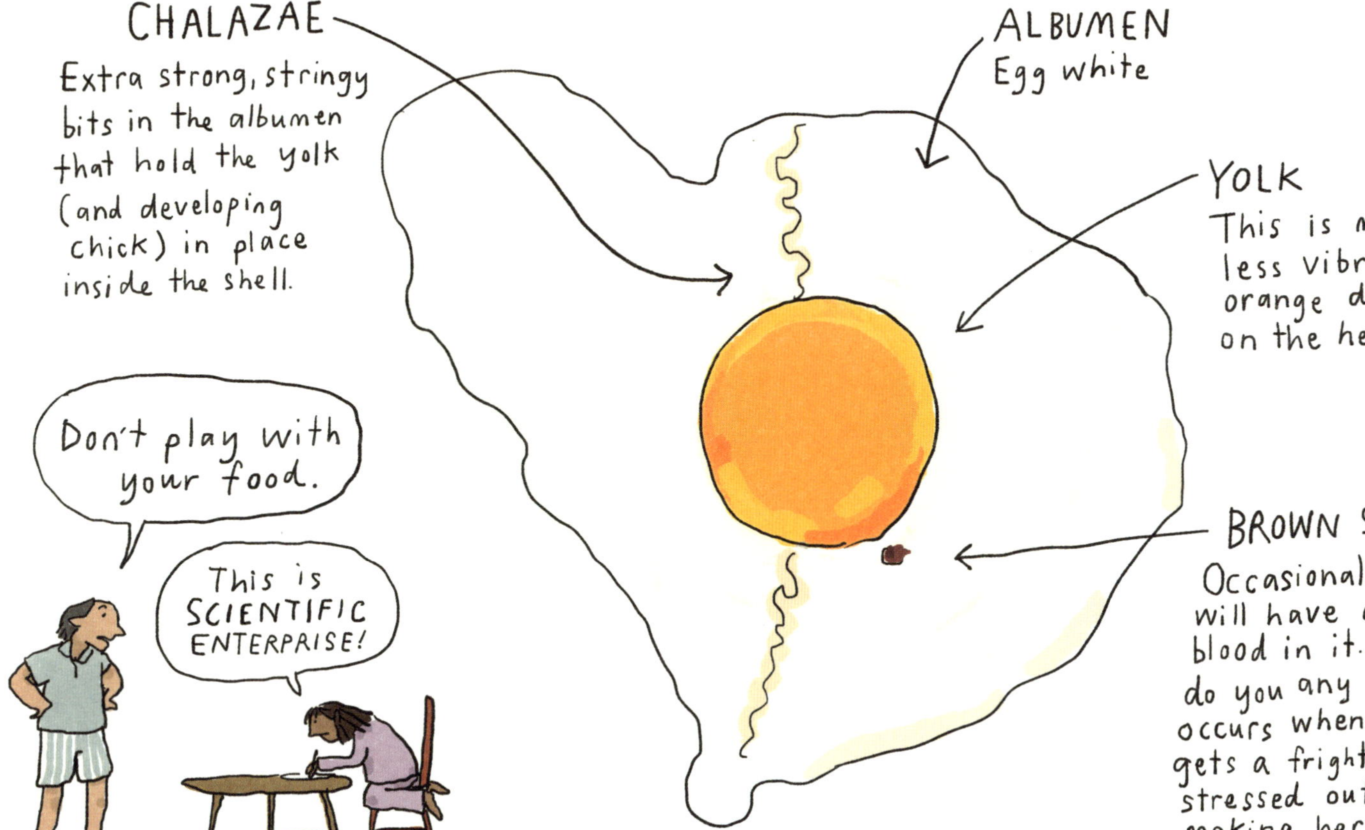

THE IMPORTANT BUSINESS OF BIRDS

Frankly, thank goodness for birds. Without them, whole forests would die, animals would starve, the world would smell terrible and we'd feel a bit lonely.

If you've ever looked at a bird and thought, "What ARE you doing, funny creature?," here are some answers it might give you.

POLLINATION

Pollination isn't just the business of insects! Birds that drink nectar from flowers also spread pollen around, allowing those flowers to make seeds.

Some flowers can only be pollinated by birds—sometimes just a single species of bird.

SPREADING SEEDS

One strategy that plants use for spreading their seeds is to offer birds a delicious sugary meal. When birds gobble up fruit and berries, they swallow seeds too, which don't break down in the bird's stomach. Then the bird flies off and poops them out somewhere else, giving the plant not just a new place to grow but a nice lump of fertilizer as well.

FERTILIZING

Bird poop, or guano, is full of nutrients. For many plants, it's a powerful fertilizer, giving them what they need to grow big and lush. Seabird colonies can be surrounded by beautiful flower gardens. When rain washes the guano into the sea, it feeds gardens of seaweed too.

BEING EDIBLE

Birds are part of the food chain, and there are other animals that need to eat them! This is the way nature works, even though it's sad to think about. When you like a particular animal, it's easy to see its natural predators as baddies, but they're just living their lives in the only way they can.

CLEANING

Carrion-eating birds clean up the bodies of dearly departed animals so they're not just lying around being stinky. Little birds eat mosquitos, maggots and slugs...all of which are good creatures that have their place in the world, but it IS possible to have too much of a good thing.

WHAT TO CALL A BIRD

This is my friend Gerald.

No... that's my friend Arthur.

A single species of bird often has a bunch of different names. Not like a spy with secret identities, more like someone with a lot of different groups of friends who each call them by a different nickname.

Firstly, they'd get named by the people native to the same place as the bird. Birds that are native to lots of areas would get a name given to them in each place.

Then, when people from other parts of the world came along, they'd see the birds for the first time and give them another name. They tended to give the birds names based on what they already knew from their own country. That's how we got two different kinds of magpie, even though they're not at all closely related.

Finally, scientists give each species a unique scientific name so that in formal situations we can all agree we're discussing the same animal. They're usually two (sometimes three) words, and they're based on Greek or Latin.

EURASIAN MAGPIE
Pica pica

AUSTRALIAN MAGPIE
Gymnorhina tibicen

There are lots of birds with common names that sound like their call. Like kākā, chickadees and kittiwakes.

Scientific names aren't as tricky to say as they first appear. Even the really impossible-looking ones aren't so bad if you break them up into pieces. But most of them are much easier than that!

Say them confidently, and if you don't get them quite right it doesn't matter—there's nothing embarrassing about a bit of trial and error. If anyone makes fun of you, then they're being a *megacephalus*.

As you get familiar with scientific names, you'll start to notice fragments of words that are often used. Then you can decode their meanings.

chloro or viridis	green
albus or leuco	white
niger or melano	black
flavus or crocos	yellow
brunneus or fuscus	brown
caeruleus or cyano	blue
erythro or ruber	red
purpureus	purple

rhynchus	beak
cephalo	head
ptero	wing
ops	eye
pod	foot
cerco	tail
pennis	feather

frugivorus	fruit-eating
troglodytes	cave-dweller
vol	flying
platy	flat
brachy	short
bi	two
micro	small
mega	large
poly	lots

languida	relaxed
eu	good
importunus	annoying
ferox	fierce
magnificens	magnificent
domesticus	tame

BIRDS AFTER DARK

It's easy to imagine birds all tucked up in comfy nests at night, but that only happens when they're sitting on eggs or chicks.

Birds need to sleep somewhere as safe as possible from predators. Tall trees or dense twiggy bushes are good options for small perching birds. Other birds sleep on the ground in big groups, so there's always someone to raise the alarm if they sense danger.

Birds that live in flocks make a real ruckus when they're getting ready for bed. They have a LOT to discuss with each other before they go to sleep, and immediately after waking up (at the first hint of daylight).

Being able to fly gives birds the option of roaming freely around the planet. Flying across entire oceans and continents is really risky though, so they don't do it just for a summer trip. Fruit and insects are scarce in winter, so birds that eat those things need to follow the warmer weather.

For bar-tailed godwits, that means flying non-stop all the way from Alaska to New Zealand. They can't float or swim, so they can't take a break on the water, but that doesn't mean that they're going for weeks without sleeping! Birds can put just half their brain to sleep at a time, leaving the other half free to think about flying, floating, standing on one leg and not falling out of trees.

Nocturnal birds operate differently to diurnal birds. Some of them have extraordinary night vision for navigating and finding food in the pitch dark, but others (like kiwi) follow their noses instead. Super sensitive hearing can be the difference between enjoying a meal or being a meal, which makes the ability to creep around in silence equally as important (see barn owls on page 83).

Being diurnal humans, we lack good night vision or exceptional nostrils, so it can be difficult to investigate birds after dark. But our ears, while not quite up to an owl's specifications, are perfectly suitable for the job. Listen carefully for birds calling at night, or for a sudden rustle when you walk past a hedge that little birds are roosting in.

A lot of seabirds are most active at night. They'll wait until the local birds of prey have gone to bed before they come ashore to their nests, then leave again at the crack of dawn.

To stay warm while they sleep, birds fluff up their feathers (to trap more air between them) and tuck their head under one of their wings. If they've got a short neck, they can just slouch.

Standing on one leg can keep birds warm as less of their skin is exposed. It's like pulling your hands up inside your sleeves on a chilly day.

NIGHTJARS

Nightjars are nocturnal birds with tiny beaks and a GAPING MAW for a mouth. Another name for nightjars is goatsuckers—2000 years ago someone decided that these birds were creeping around at night suckling milk from their goats without permission.

What they actually like eating is insects. They're crepuscular hunters, because they're not that good at seeing in the dark.

Another fantastic fact about nightjars is that they have a pectinate claw on their middle toe. It looks like a little built-in moustache comb, and it's likely the birds use it for feather maintenance.

"Pectinate" means shaped like a comb or rake. →

NESTS

If you live somewhere with a lot of deciduous trees that lose their leaves over winter, the best time to look for bird nests is when the branches are bare. You can spot the dense clumps of last summer's nests. Or a blustery storm might knock them to the ground. The nests won't be in use at that time of year, so it's okay for you to look closely at the design and what they're made of. You might be able to guess what sort of bird made the nest, and next spring you can watch to see if those birds return to the same tree to make fresh nests.

If you're especially observant and spot a bird's nest during breeding season, back away and only keep watch from afar. The parent birds will need to come and go freely to get food for themselves and their chicks, and they'll be too afraid if you're right there.

Try weaving a few twigs and pieces of grass together and you'll be in awe of how clever birds are. And they have to do it with their mouths!

BUILDING MATERIALS

You can leave nice bits and pieces lying around during nesting season and wait for birds to carry them away.

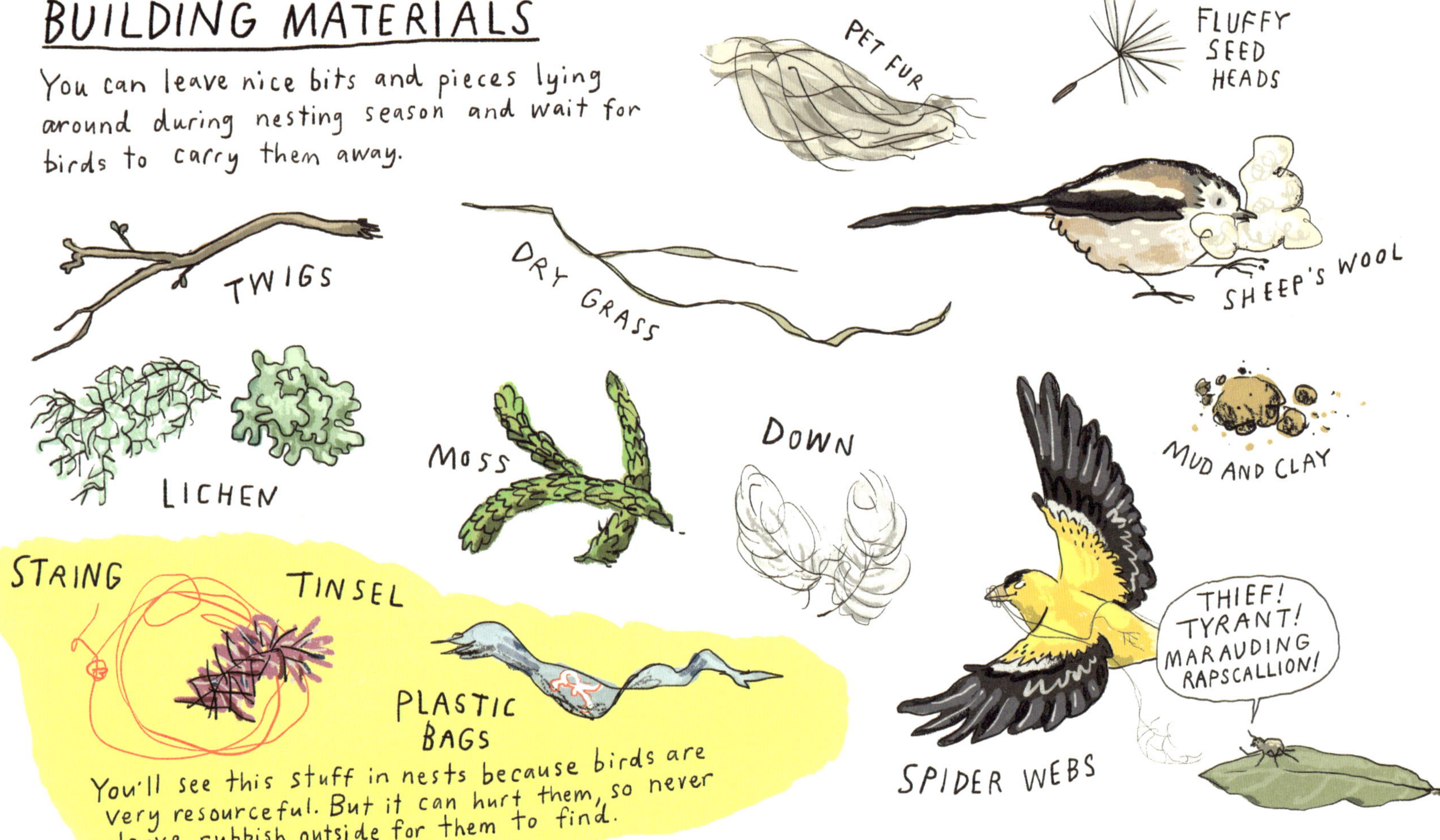

SONG THRUSH

A carefully woven basket with a smooth mud bowl inside, only about a grown-up's height off the ground.

STARLING

Starlings will build their nests in any snug hole they can find.

FLAMINGO

A mud castle on the ground near the water, tall enough to keep the egg and chick dry.

EUROPEAN GOLDFINCH

A snuggly cup made mostly from anything soft and fluffy.

HOUSE SPARROW

Large and loose, made from long pieces of dry grass. Built in very high branches.

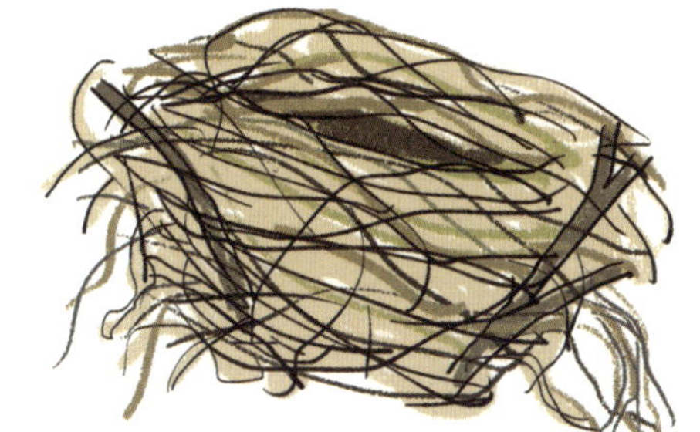

(They'll also build nests in found holes, like starlings.)

BANDED DOTTEREL

Nothing more than a little dip in the beach pebbles — almost invisible!

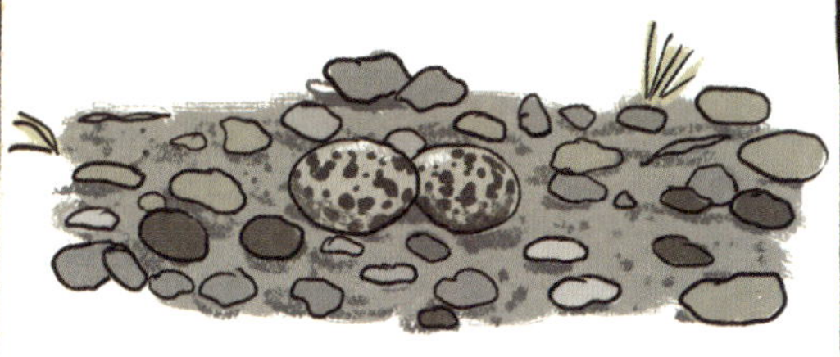

SWALLOW

Made from lots of mud like a pottery bowl. Built in sheltered nooks like a cave or an old shed.

ADÉLIE PENGUIN

A pile of little rocks. These make good nests in Antarctica because they allow snow and ice to drain away.

Collecting enough pebbles is hard work so penguins will steal from other penguins' piles when they can.

LONG-TAILED TIT

An extremely snug design with walls and a roof. Uses lots of lichen, feathers and cobwebs.

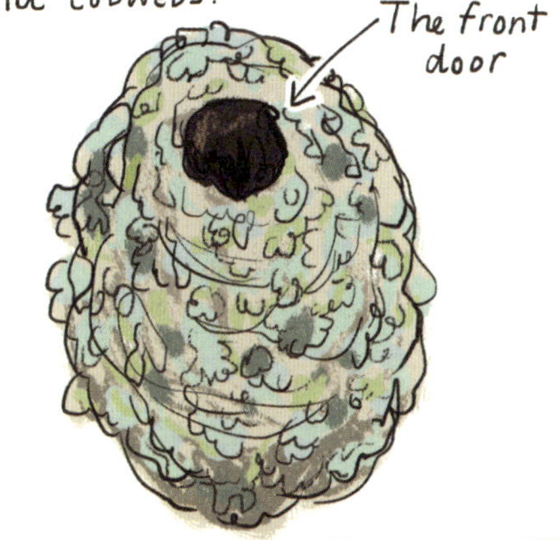

NEW BIRDS

New birds come in two styles: some chicks hatch ready to run and fend for themselves, while others seem only half formed. A fluffy new chicken can find its own food and manage quite a lot for itself but is also easy to lose. A bald little pigeon needs more help from its parents in the nest—but the extra time being looked after allows it to develop a bigger brain.

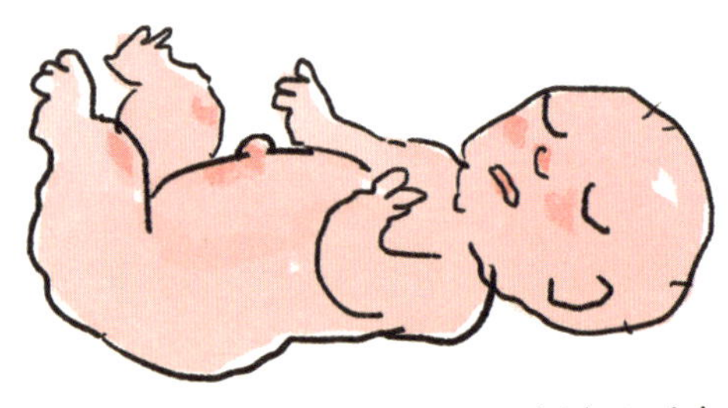

ANOTHER ALTRICIAL ANIMAL

You're telling me you have to wait EIGHTEEN years???

Megapodes are unusual because they're SUPERprecocial. They can fly on the same day they hatch and don't need their parents at all.

Kiwi chicks don't have an egg tooth, they kick their way into the world instead.

Getting out of an egg is a specialist skill and you need the right tools. Most birds use an egg tooth. It's an extra sharp little nubbin on top of their beak, just for hatching. It falls off about a day after they've made their grand entrance.

OLD BIRDS

If they don't get ill or snaffled by a predator, birds can live a really long time, often a lot longer than we realize. (Even if you saw a wild cockatoo one day and saw it again five years later, you wouldn't know it was the same one because they all look so alike.) Some species of birds live so long they were just chicks when your grandparents were babies.

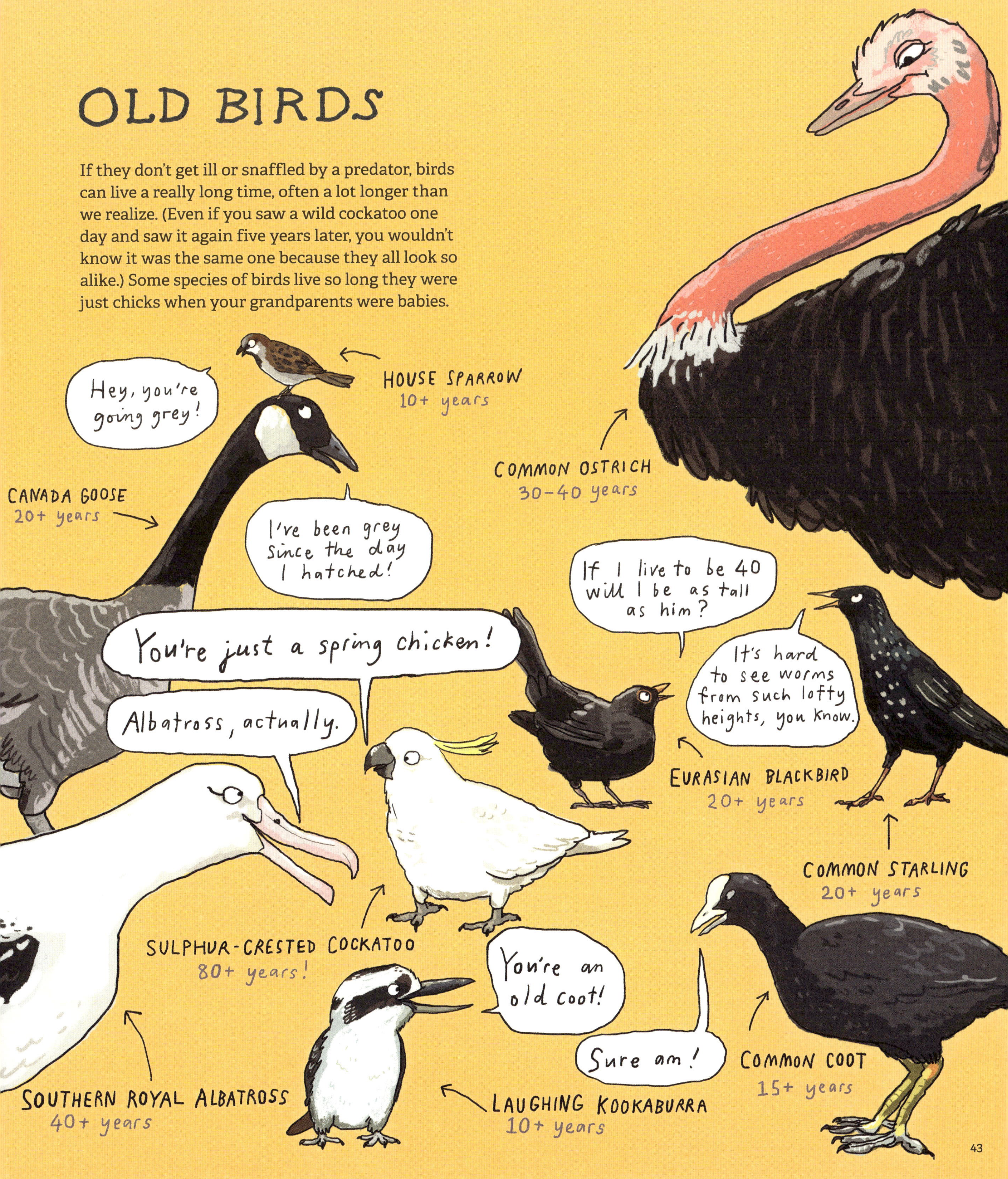

CURIOUS DEPOSITS
FROM THE FRONT

We tend to think of our own mouths as, at least ideally, one-way systems. Not so for birds, who have as many good reasons to vomit as they do to swallow.

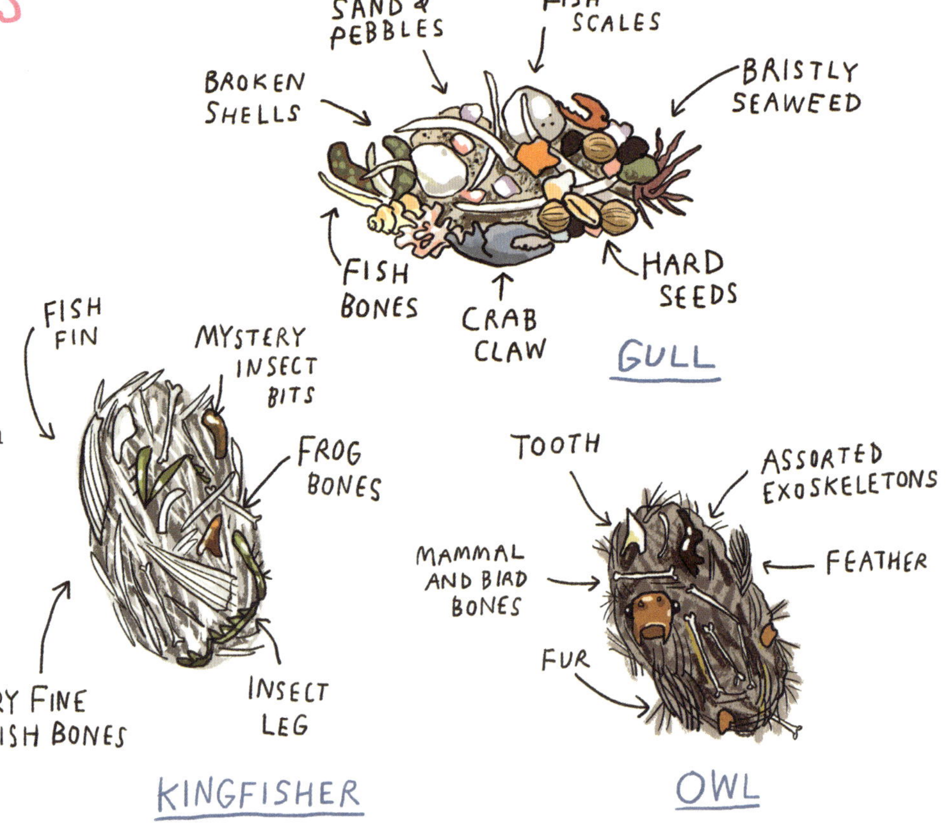

PELLETS

Birds that eat a diet of crunchy insects, shellfish and bony little critters end up swallowing a lot of things they can't actually digest—shells, fur, teeth, that sort of thing. Instead of pooping all this out, they bring it up in reverse, producing what we call a pellet. Pellets are absolutely fascinating.

BABY FOOD

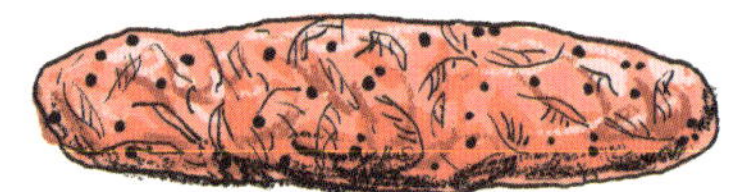

A delicious krill sausage made with a mother prion's love

Land birds can go back and forth from the nest with caterpillars and worms in their beaks all day, but seabirds make one big trip at a time. They swallow krill, squid or little fish and then regurgitate (that's a polite word for vomit) it for their chicks later.

DEFENSIVE BARFING

A seabird chick left on its own can't do much to protect itself from predators, but some CAN projectile vomit on them as a deterrent.

GIZZARD STONES

Birds that eat particularly tough and chewy meals use gizzard stones to help digest their food. These can be tiny pebbles for turkeys, or bits the size of driveway gravel for emus and emperor penguins.

The birds swallow the stones, and they settle in the bird's gizzard where strong muscles churn them around, grinding up big bits of food as they go. Instead of chewing their food before swallowing, they chew it after swallowing!

Gizzard stones get worn smooth over time and need replacing with fresh, coarse ones. If you're lucky, you might see a bird vomit up its used gizzard stones and you can go admire the little pile it leaves behind.

Depending on where the bird lives, its stones could be very pretty.

FROM THE BACK

Bird droppings are called guano, and guano can tell you so much more than you might think. Without even laying eyes on the bird, you can guess its size, where it lives and what it eats.

Birds poop a lot more often than mammals, so if there are any birds around at all, there will be plops.

A SEABIRD OR A GULL

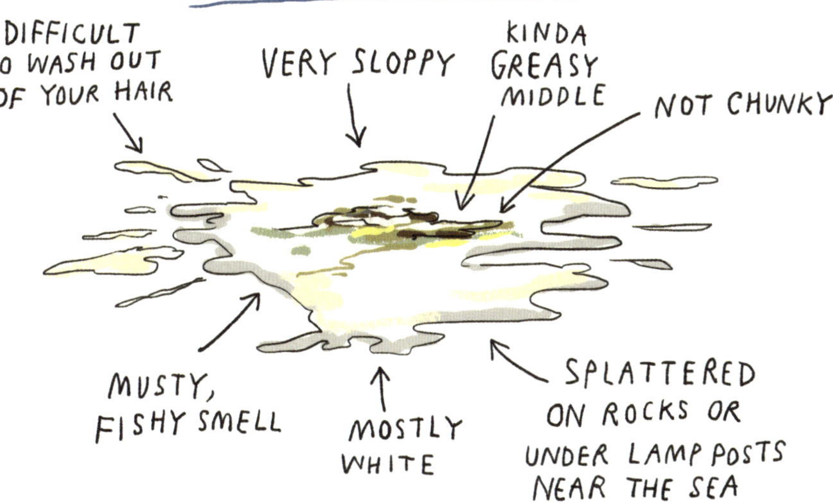

LARGE WATERFOWL (LIKE A GOOSE OR SWAN)

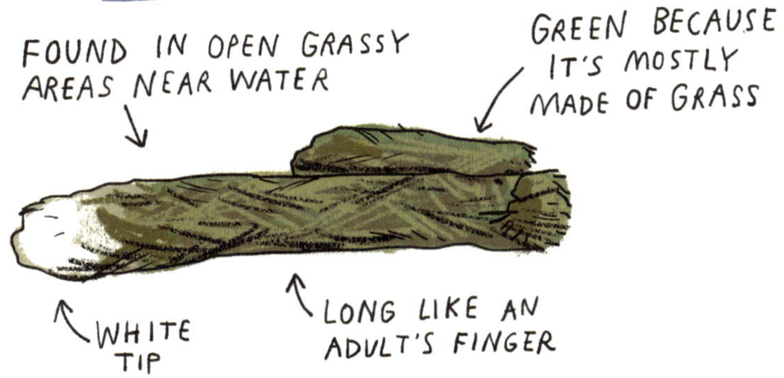

A SMALL SEED-EATING BIRD (LIKE A SPARROW OR FINCH)

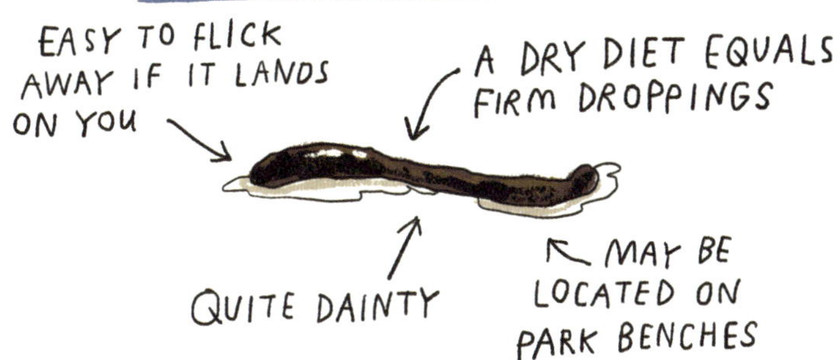

A FRUIT EATER (LIKE A BLACKBIRD OR WOOD PIGEON)

HOME HYGIENE

Birds don't poop in their nests if they can help it. When nestlings need to make a deposit, it comes out of their bottoms neatly wrapped in a thin membrane called a fecal sac. Their parents can pick this up and cart it away to be smelly somewhere else.

STINKY LEGS

Some birds poop on their own legs on purpose to cool down in hot weather. It's called urohidrosis when this stork does it. It's probably called something else when your baby brother does it.

How to Usher a Bird Outdoors

1. Most importantly, get everyone to stay really quiet and still. The best thing is to free the bird without ever touching it.

2. Turn off any lights inside—the bird will look for bright light to guide itself to freedom.

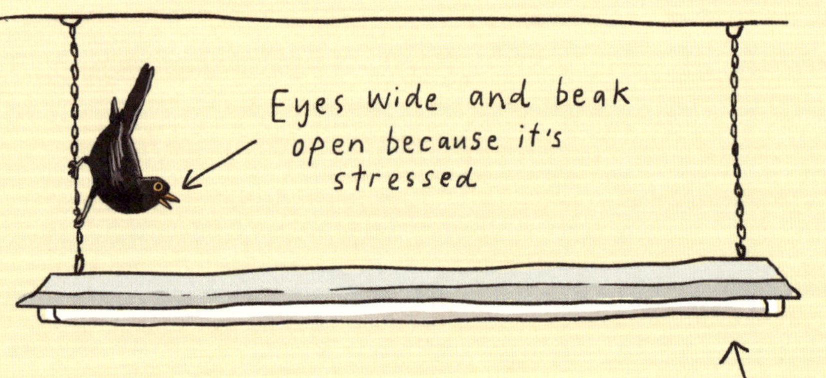

Terrified birds do a lot of poops, so the quieter and calmer you act around the bird, the less poop you'll have to clean off your books later.

3. If possible, close the curtains or blinds on all the windows except for one, and open that one window as wide as you can.

4. Be patient. The bird will be freaking out thinking it's about to die, and it can't be reasoned with. Stay calm and let the bird find the bright, open window in its own time.

NOTES FROM 18 INVESTIGATIONS

DUCKS

No park ever really seems complete without a pond full of ducks. The species you see just about everywhere is the mallard duck.

Ducks that dabble and tug at slippery water weeds have pointy little tomia (beaks with jagged edges) for grip—you can imagine how hard it'd be to eat otherwise.

Mallards are dabbling ducks, not diving ducks. Instead of swimming underwater, they just tip their bums up in the air like buoys while they reach for whatever tasty morsels they can find below them. They eat plants, worms, swimming insects and seeds.

It's very tempting to feed ducks, but they need food that won't make them sick. Despite their enthusiasm for bread, it's actually really bad for them.

GOOD FOOD FOR DUCKS

Most birds mate by kissing their butts together, cloaca to cloaca. Ducks are notable for doing it differently, since the males actually have penises (hardly any birds have these). They're shaped like corkscrews and resemble an octopus tentacle.

A HANDSOME CHAP

A MALLARD DRAKE IN HIS BREEDING PLUMAGE

Feathers that shine emerald green in the sunlight

Thinking about that lovely puddle he saw yesterday

Chubby cheeks

Drakes have higher-pitched, raspier voices than hens. Only female mallards say "QUACK!"

Bill as yellow as a marigold

Elegant neck

This lump on the tip is called a nail.

Crisp white collar

When ducks settle down comfortably or tuck their heads under their wing for a snooze like this, it's called loafing.

Female mallards build secretive nests in long vegetation close to water. They pluck out some of their own down to make the nest soft. They don't always get the secretive part right though.

Big flappy feet are fantastic for paddling in water and walking on swampy ground, but most ducks can't grip onto branches well enough to sit in trees. The wood duck is one of the few duck species that can, because they have extra-long, sharp claws. They make their nests in holes in trees.

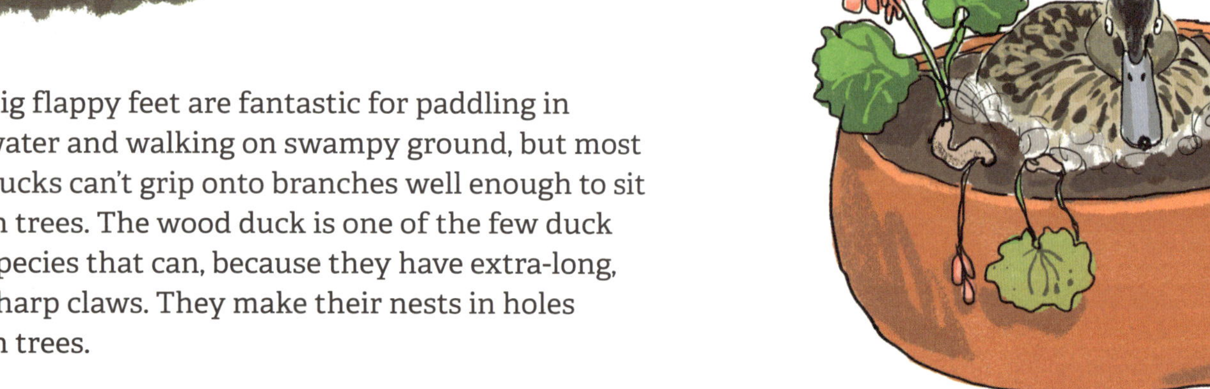

CURIOUS DUCKS OF THE WORLD

A male mute swan can weigh up to 15 kilograms, which is very heavy for a flying bird.
Imagine trying to keep three sacks of flour airborne.
Big webbed palmate paddles on short, sturdy legs

SWANS

If a giraffe could be compared to a stretched-out horse, and an alpaca to an extended sheep, a swan could be seen as an elongated duck. Why have so many different animals evolved spectacular serpentine necks? To reach food that less necky animals can't. For swans, this means being able to graze underwater plants without having to dive.

I politely request that you examine your harmful prejudices.

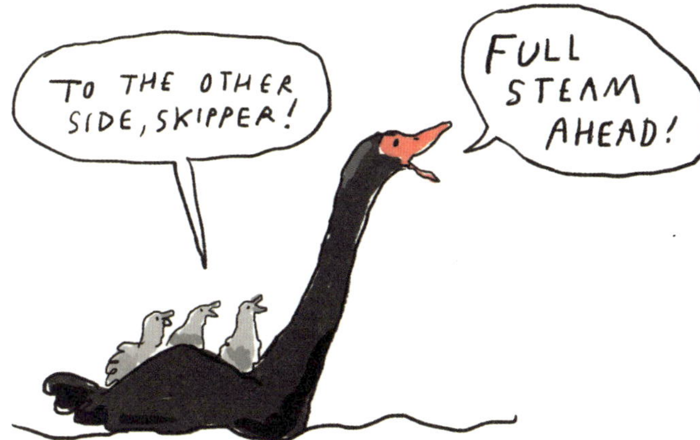

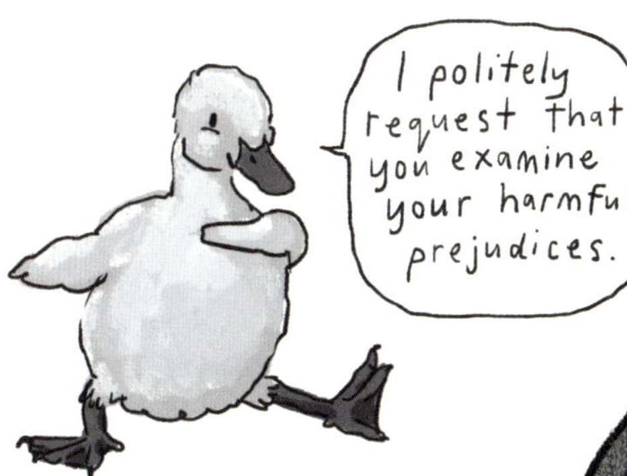

A male swan is called a cob, and a female swan is called a pen. A baby swan is called a cygnet, and it's just as cute as any duckling.

TO THE OTHER SIDE, SKIPPER!
FULL STEAM AHEAD!

When cygnets are very little, they can hitch a ride upon their own private cruise ship.

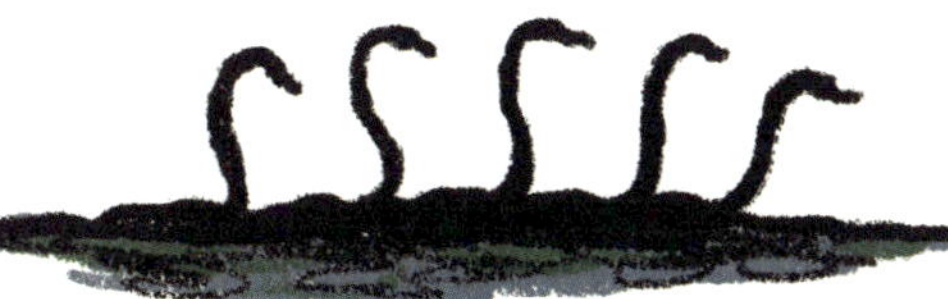

From far away a group of swimming swans looks like a sea monster.

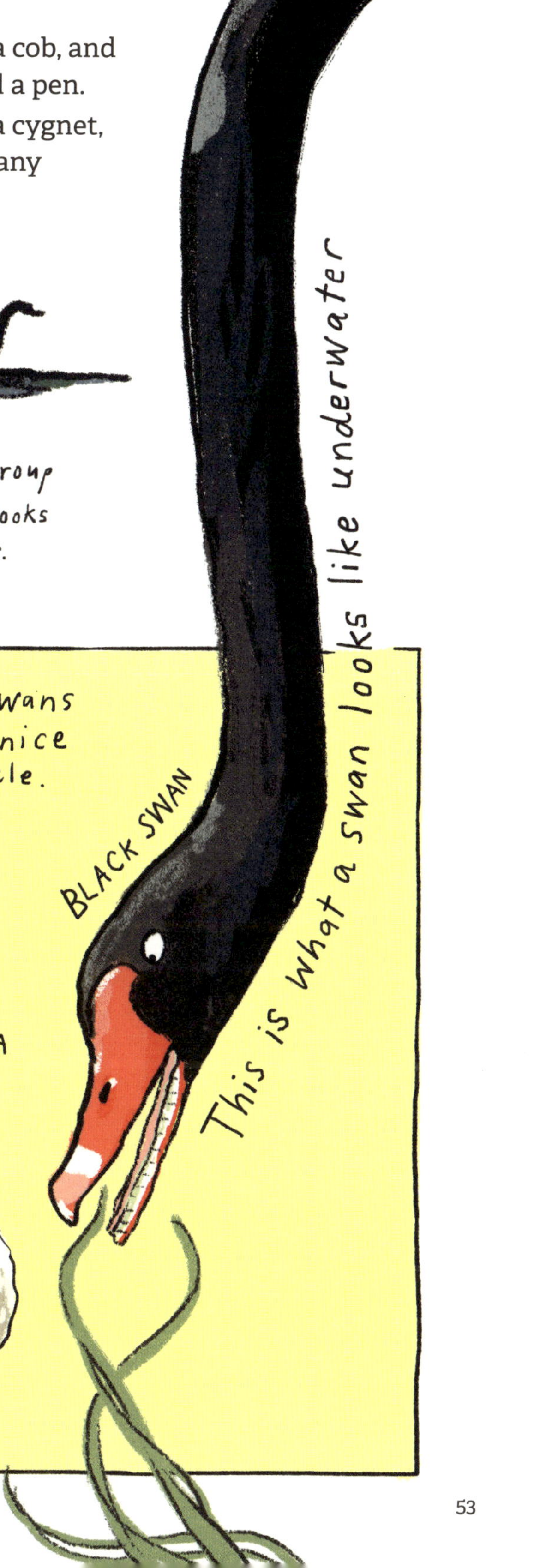
This is what a swan looks like underwater

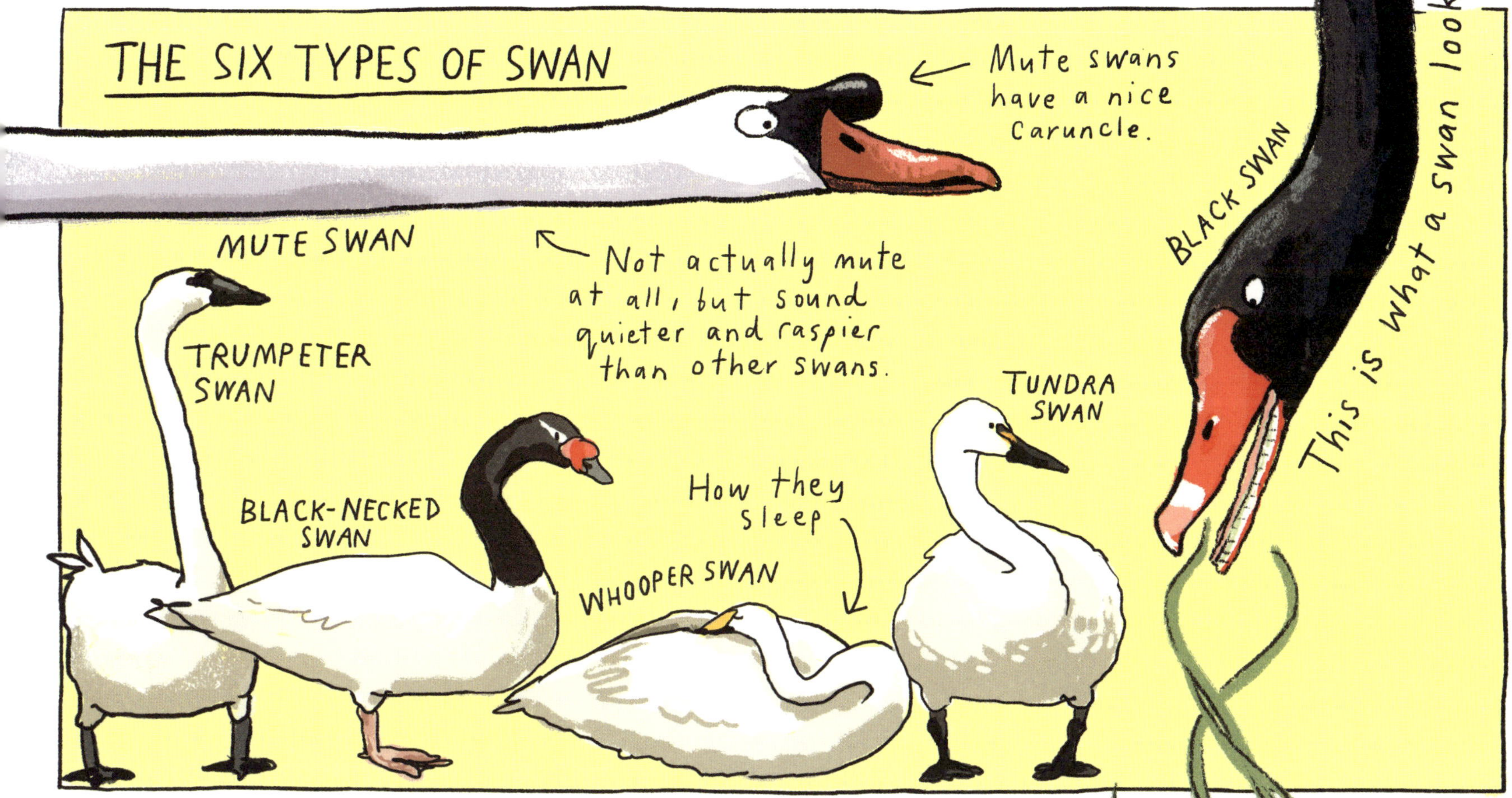
THE SIX TYPES OF SWAN
Mute swans have a nice caruncle.
MUTE SWAN
Not actually mute at all, but sound quieter and raspier than other swans.
BLACK SWAN
TRUMPETER SWAN
TUNDRA SWAN
BLACK-NECKED SWAN
How they sleep
WHOOPER SWAN

GULLS

If you're being really fussy about it, there's no such thing as a SEAgull. And not all gulls are seabirds. Although they often live on the coast, they're happy in all kinds of places.

A lot of people think gulls are annoying because the common species are noisy and want to join in when we have hot chips and picnics on the beach. We have a lot in common, if you think about it.

Some gulls have this red spot on their beak. Chicks tap at it when they want the adult to regurgitate food for them. It's like a big, red vending machine button (but the only thing you can order is leftovers).

Gulls get uncomfortably bulgy necks when their crop is full of something (or someone) they swallowed whole.

EXCUSE ME! CAN ANYONE HELP ME?

Gull chicks are precocial, but unlike ducklings, most of them won't go swimming until they have proper feathers. They run around more like baby chickens, using their speckled camouflage to hide.

Gulls nest in colonies, so when the chicks are young, all the adult birds work together to protect them. When birds do this, it's called crèching.

If you see gulls slapping their feet on the ground like this, they're teasing little worms and crabs to the surface.

Wet sand or mud

Watch out for gulls suspended casually in mid air. They hold their wings out and use their tail feathers for balance, staying aloft on warm air currents called thermals. It's terrifically clever.

← A THERMAL
(The same air movement that glider pilots use to stay up)

TAWAKI
Eudyptes pachyrhynchus
Lay their eggs in nooks and burrows under lush rainforest
When it's not nesting season, penguins can spend so long in the sea that barnacles grow on their tails.

PENGUINS

It's funny how we think of penguins as wintry animals, when really almost none of them live on ice. Out of all 18 penguin species, only five live on the Antarctic continent (that includes the Antarctic peninsula, which sticks out quite far north and isn't all that icy). Only emperor and Adélie penguins truly live on or among the ice; the others prefer lush forests and even tropical islands.

All wild penguins live in the Southern Hemisphere. Galápagos penguins live so close to the equator that they'll sometimes swim into the Northern Hemisphere though.

KING PENGUIN
Aptenodytes patagonicus

King penguin chicks look so unlike the adults that people once thought they were a different species altogether, which they named the woolly penguin.

SNARES PENGUIN
Eudyptes robustus

Snares penguins are quite adept at climbing trees.

NORTHERN ROCKHOPPER
Eudyptes moseleyi

Rockhopper penguins have the most flamboyantly wonderful eyebrows of any seabird.

MAGELLANIC PENGUIN
Spheniscus magellanicus

Early European explorers who'd never seen a penguin before thought Magellanic penguins were a type of goose. Perhaps they'd never seen a goose before either.

African penguins live in Namibia and South Africa, where it can be sweltering hot. Sometimes they're called jackass penguins because they sound like donkeys.

AFRICAN PENGUIN
Spheniscus demersus

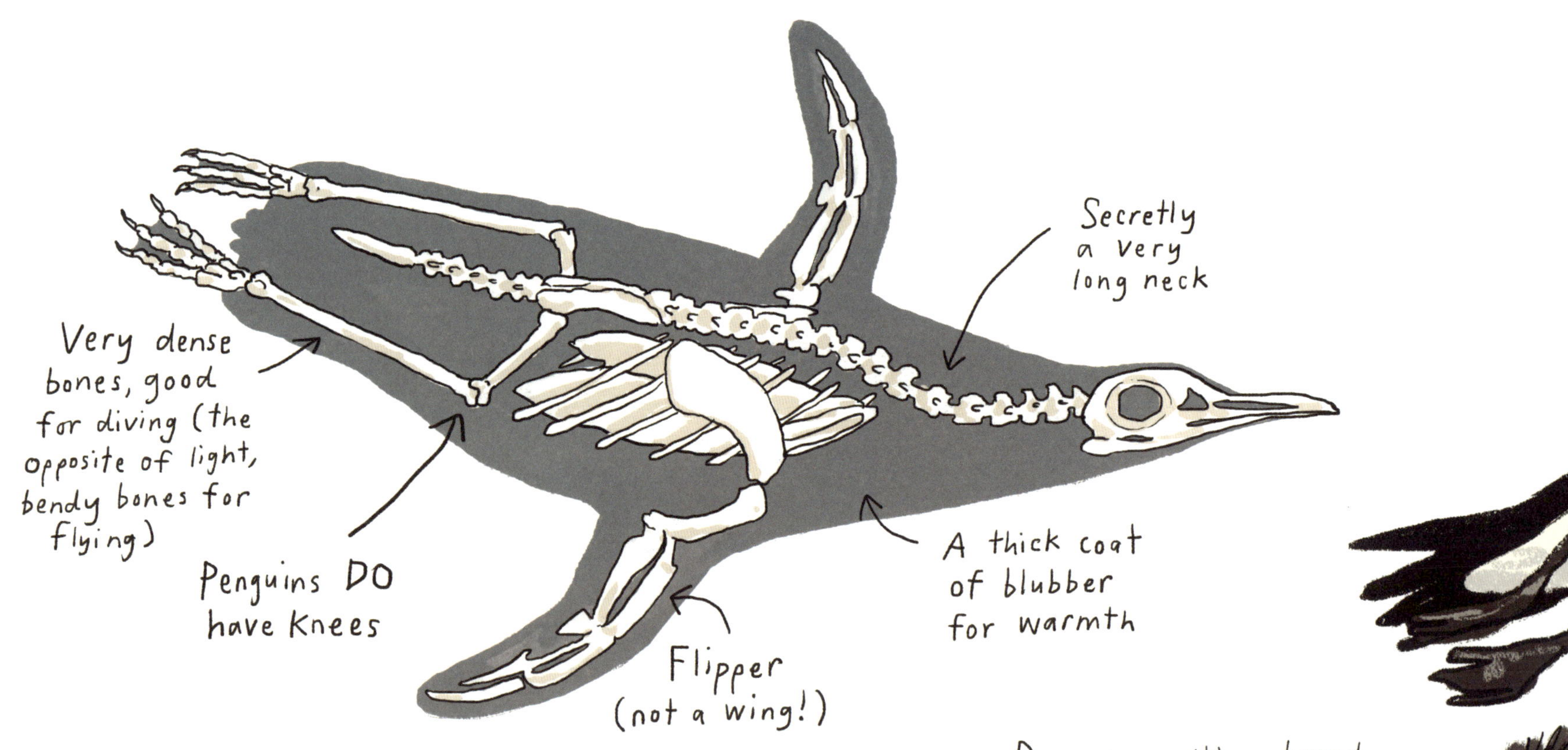

You can guess the temperature of a penguin by how pink its feet are. Because their bodies are like insulated wetsuits, it's easy for them to overheat when the sun's out, but they have a trick for this. They direct their blood flow to patches of bare skin—on their flippers, their feet and (for African or Galápagos penguins) their faces. Pumping blood to these exposed spots means a breeze can cool it down, lowering the penguin's overall body temperature. So a cold penguin has greyish feet and a hot penguin has pink feet full of blood!

Penguins with a broad, robust bill eat a lot of krill and squid.

And a hooked tip is useful for climbing rocks.

Penguins with slender bills mainly eat fish.

Weeeeeeeee!

Walking turns into waddling when your knees are tucked way up under your belly, and if you've got a long way to go then tobogganing is much better. Penguins in Antarctica use their feet, flippers and smooth bellies to scooch comfortably across the ice.

BIRDS OF THE NORTHERN HEMISPHERE THAT LOOK A BIT PENGUINY BUT AREN'T PENGUINS
RAZORBILL
Alca torda
LOOK! A FLYING PENGUIN!
Just kidding!
DOVEKIE
Alle alle
~~TUFTY PUFF~~ TUFTED PUFFIN
Fratercula cirrhata
A lot of birds have beaks that look quite frowny to us. Not this one!
ATLANTIC PUFFIN
Fratercula arctica
PARAKEET AUKLET
Aethia psittacula
COMMON MURRE
Uria aalge

SEABIRD SPOTTING

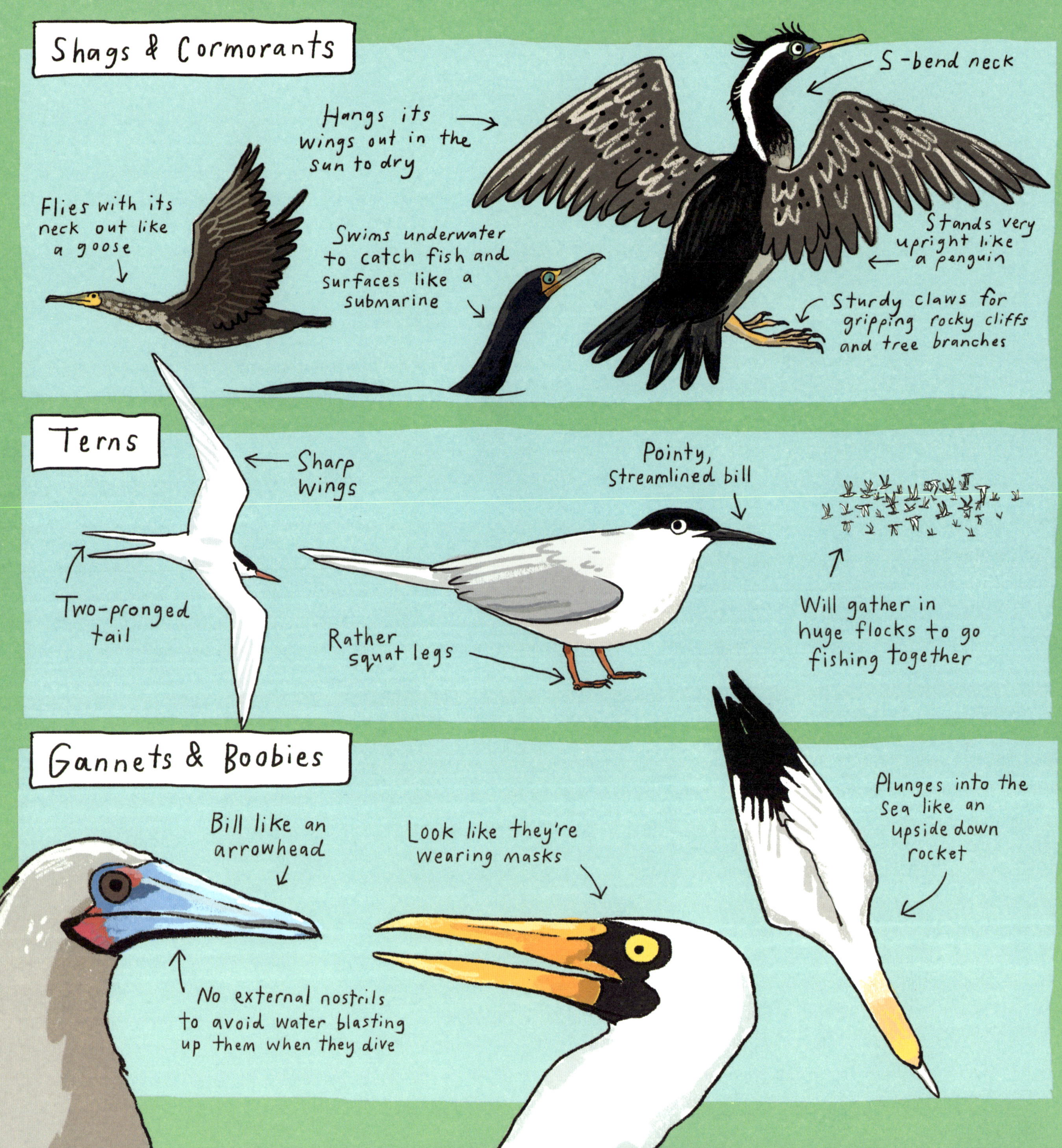

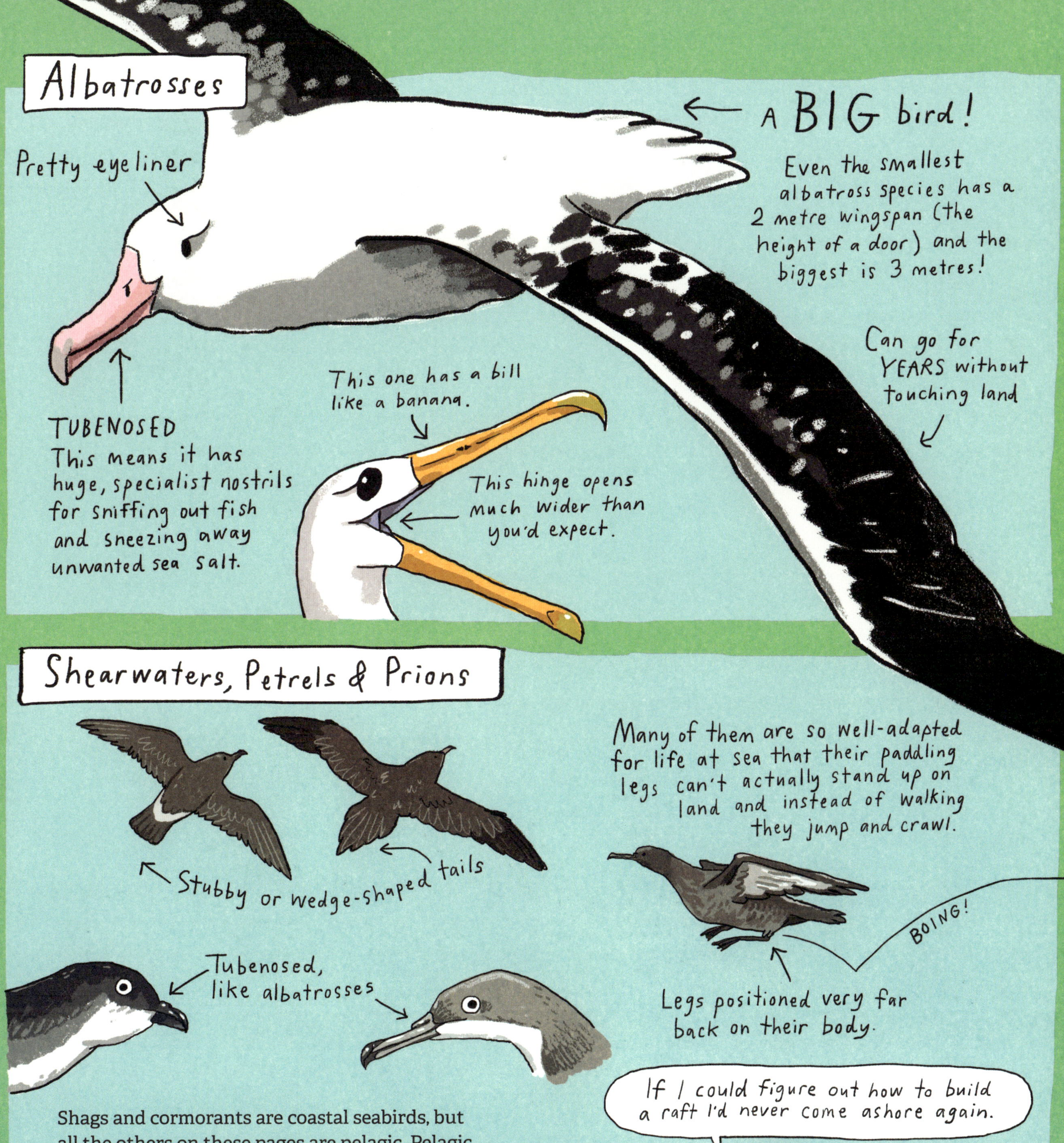

Shags and cormorants are coastal seabirds, but all the others on these pages are pelagic. Pelagic seabirds live most of their lives on the ocean a really long way from land. The only reason they come to shore is to breed and raise their chicks.

It looks like pigeons bob their heads when they walk, but technically their heads stay still while their bodies move. They do this to keep their eyes stable and keep a better watch on food and predators. We don't need to move like that because our eyes move in their sockets instead.

Columba livia domestica

FERAL PIGEONS

FERAL = An animal that was domesticated but now lives in the wild

WILD = Wild!

The pigeons we see everywhere are the descendants of wild rock doves that were tamed by humans thousands of years ago, then escaped from their cages or were abandoned. Wild rock doves still exist, but there's not many of them left because feral pigeons have taken over.

There isn't really any difference between what we call pigeons and doves. They're both just common names for birds in the same family, Columbidae. But we tend to think of doves as being pretty and clean. Pigeons don't enjoy such a good reputation and often get called rats with wings, which is entirely unfair to pigeons AND rats, who each have their own fine qualities.

Keep an eye out for pigeons with different patterns in their feathers. Domestic pigeons were bred to be all kinds of pretty shades, so fancy plumage still pops up among the feral population.

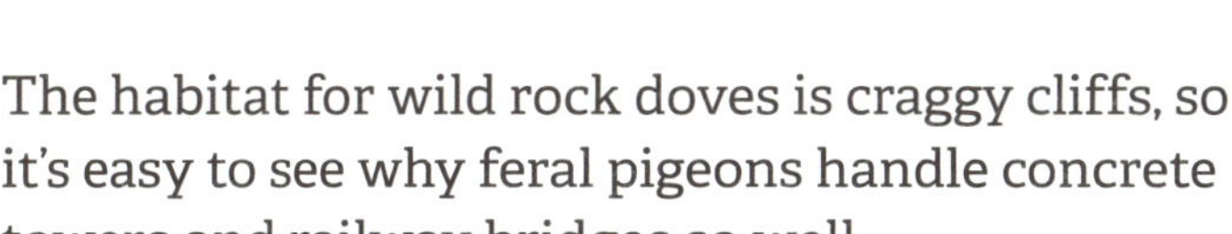

The habitat for wild rock doves is craggy cliffs, so it's easy to see why feral pigeons handle concrete towers and railway bridges so well.

CROP MILK

Pigeons make milk, but not the sort you'd want to put in your hot chocolate. It's made in their crop, and it resembles a soft yellow cheese. They regurgitate it for their wee squabs to eat.

Pigeons aren't known for their nest-building skills. But there are over 100 million feral pigeons in the world, so it seems like they know what they're doing.

CORVIDS

The *Corvus* genus includes rooks, ravens and crows, which all look pretty similar. They're all black with big beaks, but you can spot the differences if you take the time to look carefully.

The call of a crow is often used in movies to make places feel spooky, but crows aren't spooky! People even call a group of them "a murder of crows." This isn't very fair because corvids are exceptionally clever birds, and they can be sweet and generous too. If you're always really nice to the crows that live nearby, they'll bring you gifts.

The opposite is true too. If you're mean to a crow, it'll remember what you look like and scowl at you every time you walk past. What's more, that crow will tell all its friends, and they'll gang up on you. So always remember your manners.

Ruffled and bristly

Widest beak out of these three birds

Tufty

A very big bird! About the size of a well-fed house cat

RAVEN

Smaller, narrower beak

Feathery here

Very sleek

Only about as big as a feral pigeon

CROW

Pale beak

No feathers on most of its face

Bigger than a crow but smaller than a raven (just right).

ROOK

HOW TO ACT AROUND A SCARY BIRD

Now and then in life you'll meet a bird that does NOT want to be investigated. Some species can get territorial and defensive, particularly during breeding season when they're protecting eggs and chicks. Even if you're being calm and sensible and giving the bird lots of compliments, its instinct is to scare you away.

The best option is to let the bird have all the space it wants. This might mean walking a different way through the park for a few weeks until breeding season is over and the birds aren't territorial anymore.

It can be frightening if a bird swoops at you, but don't panic! Some swoopers like gulls won't really be trying to hit you, only spook you. On the other hand, Australian magpies and falcons will scrape your head if they can, so it's important to know how to defend yourself without hurting the bird.

NEVER EVER try to hit a bird, that will make everything worse.

SWOOP PROTECTION

SIGNS A BIRD IS CROSS AND YOU SHOULD STAY AWAY

HOUSE SPARROWS

It's easy for people to overlook sparrows, because they don't have bright feathers and they're always just there. Any detective worth their salt knows that the sneakiest, most interesting stuff often happens in plain sight. Sparrows are fantastic to watch. They're always doing something and chatting about it loudly.

A sparrow carrying a heavy load has to flap a lot harder than usual. Listen and you can hear the difference.

Sparrows don't scratch in the dirt for worms. Adult sparrows mostly eat seeds (or cracker crumbs and dropped sandwiches) but they can't feed those to their chicks. During nesting season, you might notice sparrows searching the eaves of houses for spiders, or hunting in trees for fat caterpillars to take back to their babies.

Town sparrows are after everyone's crumbs, so they'll hop under park benches while people are still sitting on them, or they'll wait until someone's gone to the toilet at a cafe before helping themselves to a warm scone.

Sparrows can even live happily inside very big shops.
Oranges
LAST BANANA!

STARLINGS

Common starlings are native to Europe, Asia and North Africa, which is a huge home to begin with. Then when Europeans moved to the other side of the world, they took starlings with them as pest control, to eat insects on their farms. That was silly. Now it's starlings that are considered the pests because they damage the crops! They also crowd out the native birds that should be living there.

But there's no law that says you can't enjoy watching a bird just because humans made a terrible blunder. Animals can be extraordinarily beautiful and also cause harm—both things can be true at once.

At dusk, a flock of starlings will gather in the sky above their roost and move together like a plume of dark smoke or a silk scarf blowing in the wind. It's mesmerisingly beautiful. The murmuration makes it difficult for a falcon to target and snatch a single bird, so this is probably why the starlings do it.

Starlings are mimics. They naturally make complicated whistles and clicks, but they'll also copy other birds and city noises like sirens and the beep of reversing trucks.

Starlings will eat a bit of everything—fruit, grains and nectar. But their main food sources are worms, caterpillars and grubs. They search for goodies by poking their pointy beaks into lawns and fields. You can often see the holes they've left behind.

Starlings have very fast, jerky movements. They don't pause to look and listen like blackbirds and thrushes do.

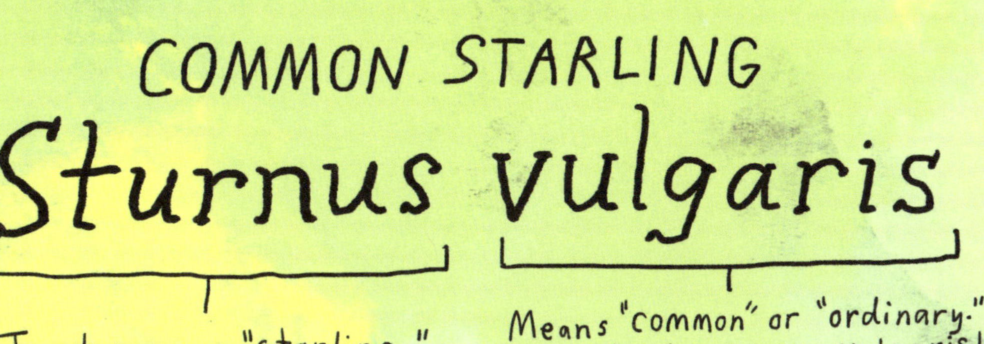

COMMON STARLING

Sturnus vulgaris

Just means "starling."

Means "common" or "ordinary." These birds are un-vulgarisly pretty, though.

Have you noticed that some birds walk and others hop? Starlings are walkers, pigeons are too. Species that spend more time in trees tend to be hoppers, like sparrows and finches.

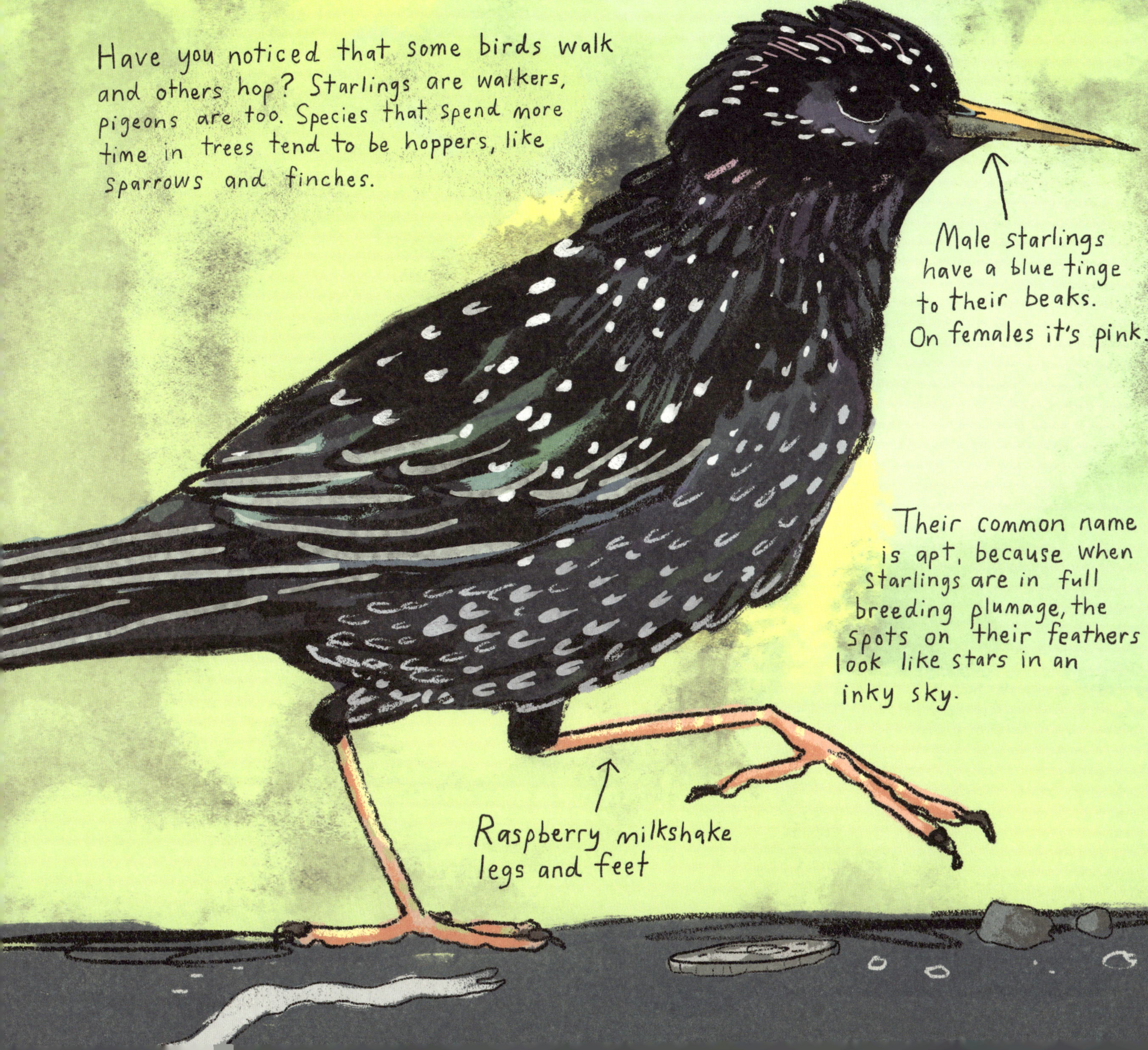

Male starlings have a blue tinge to their beaks. On females it's pink.

Their common name is apt, because when starlings are in full breeding plumage, the spots on their feathers look like stars in an inky sky.

Raspberry milkshake legs and feet

BLACKBIRDS AND THRUSHES

Blackbirds and thrushes are like cousins. They're both in the genus *Turdus*, and they have heaps of similarities. They live in the same places, like to eat most of the same things, and their nests and eggs are a lot alike.

Sometimes they're nervous nellies and won't come near you, but now and then a bold one makes friends with a gardener who throws it worms and caterpillars.

You'll often see a bunch of blackbirds or thrushes in the same place, but they don't travel in flocks.

EURASIAN BLACKBIRD
Turdus merula

Male

It seems unfair to call them blackbirds when half of them are actually brown.

Female

To save on trips to-and-from their nest they'll carry as many wriggling refreshments in their beak as they can. →

If you're watching a blackbird, you'll notice it flicking its tail up and down every so often. This is a signal that it knows you're there, and it's keeping an eye on you.

Blackbirds forage for worms and insects in the undergrowth and toss aside sticks and leaf litter with great gusto. They make more noise doing this than you'd expect from a small bird. They also leave behind bare patches where they've dug away the leaves, which you might mistake for the grubbing of a larger animal.

Because blackbirds and thrushes don't nest very high off the ground, you're quite likely to spot one. When the mother is on the nest, she'll sit very low and stay as still as she can until you go away.

As soon as a berry shows the first blush of lovely red ripeness a blackbird will swoop in to enjoy it, probably the day before you were going to pluck it for yourself.

Thrushes are specialist snail hunters. When they find one, they use rocks, bricks or concrete as anvils to crack open shells. If you find a rock surrounded by broken snail shells, this is what you've stumbled across.

How to Spot a Fledgling

A fledgling is an altricial chick that has left the nest but still needs to be fed by its parents. They're kind of like teenagers going through a bit of an awkward phase. A fledgling will be left alone for long periods of time so it might seem abandoned, but that's very unlikely. People often mistake fledglings for injured or lost chicks, but here are some clues to help you spot the difference.

The only time you should interfere with a fledgling is if it's in a really silly place, like where it could get run over. Don't pick it up, just slowly walk towards it and encourage it to hop away from you to a better spot.

Arms as wide as possible to herd it in the right direction
Creeping calmly and slowly

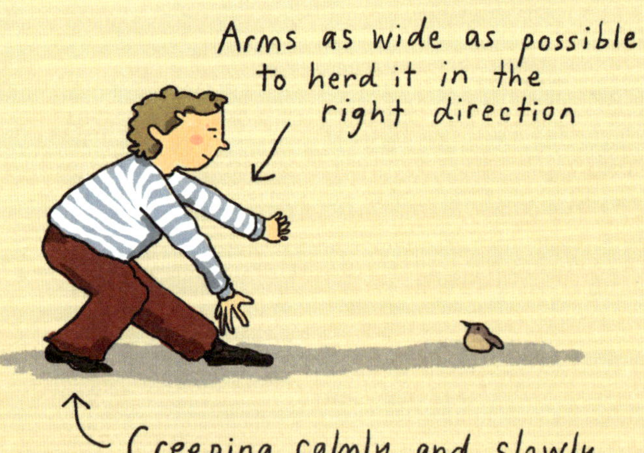

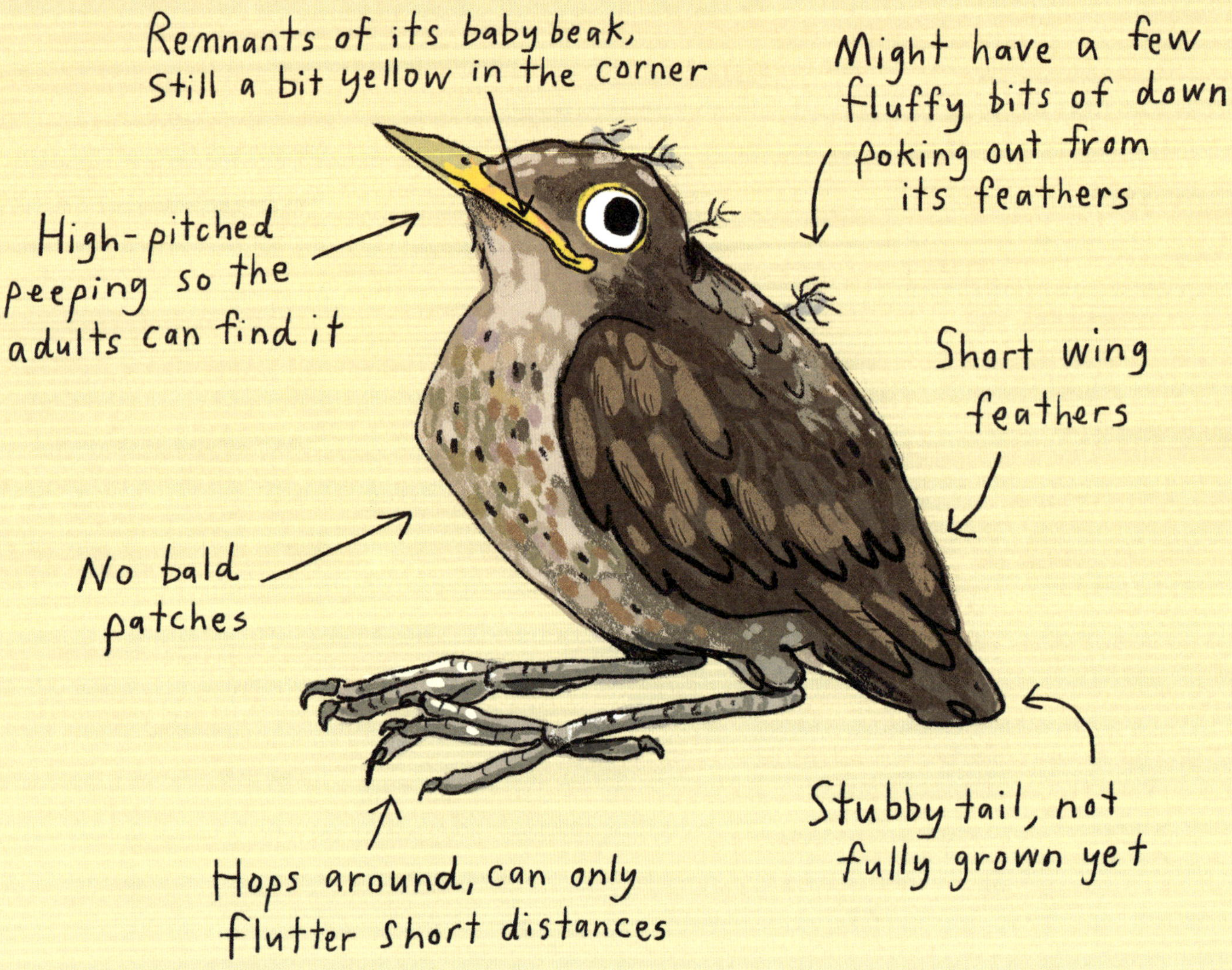
Remnants of its baby beak, still a bit yellow in the corner
Might have a few fluffy bits of down poking out from its feathers
High-pitched peeping so the adults can find it
Short wing feathers
No bald patches
Stubby tail, not fully grown yet
Hops around, can only flutter short distances

CHARMING BROWN BIRDS

Being small and speckled brown is such an excellent idea when you're a bird that rather a lot of them have evolved that way. Even the most experienced detectives may have trouble telling them apart at a glimpse, so we call them LBBs (little brown birds) or LBJs (little brown jobs). You could even call them BOIBs (birds of inconclusive brownness).

Very elongated rear talons

EURASIAN SKYLARK
Alauda arvensis

EURASIAN WREN
Troglodytes troglodytes

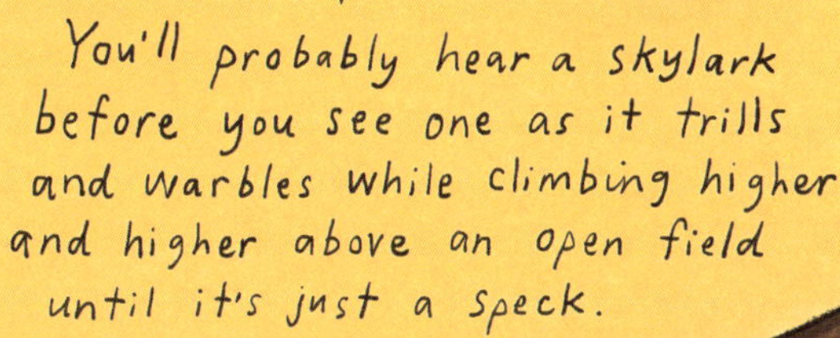

CHAFFINCH
Fringilla coelebs

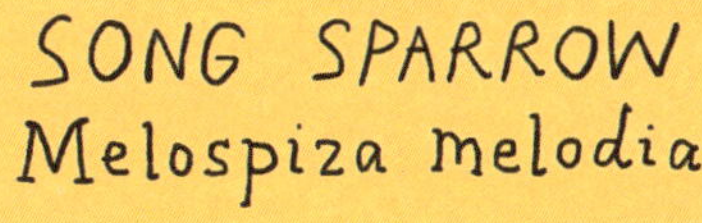

DUNNOCK
Prunella modularis

CHIPPING SPARROW
Spizella passerina

Gallus gallus
RED JUNGLEFOWL
(A WILD CHOOK)
Roosters have larger combs than hens. The redder they are, the healthier and more fertile the chicken is.
Lovely goobly wattle
Hidden ear hole
Big earlobe
Magnificently Stylish
Toes for perching
Talons for scratching up food
Spurs for fighting other roosters

CHICKENS

There are more chickens in the world than any other kind of bird because they're farmed for meat and eggs. They make wonderful pets.

Like any other animal, individual chickens have preferences, personalities and funny little quirks. You just need to get to know them.

All the chickens we farm and keep as pets are descendants of a wild bird—the red junglefowl, *Gallus gallus*.

Birds can't sweat to cool themselves down, so if they get too hot, they pant like a dog.

A wild bird would never lay eggs every day. That would use too much energy, and it would be impossible to look after that many chicks all at once! Domestic hens only do it because of thousands of years of people breeding them to be that way.

Chickens love to sunbathe. They look a little awkward when they do it, like they've pulled a muscle and can't get up.

Chickens and other birds often wipe their beaks to keep themselves tidy after eating something messy. Not only is it good manners, it might also help keep their beaks sharp.

BEAUTIFUL and SILLY CHICKEN BREEDS

Like dogs and cats, domestic chickens come in hundreds of different breeds. People who keep special breeds of domestic birds, like pigeons and chickens, are called fanciers.

Fanciers compete against each other to have the fanciest bird. They don't make them do obstacle courses though.

SEBRIGHT

TRANSYLVANIAN NAKED NECK

POLISH

MODERN GAME

BARRED ROCK

PEKIN

RUMPLESS

SERAMA

SILKIE

They peck each other's faces to fight for their position in the pecking order. It can get quite mean and leave some hens with scabbed and bloody combs.

Given half a chance, chickens chase, kill and devour small animals like mice. They look very like their dinosaur ancestors when they do it.

The pecking order is how a flock of chooks decide among themselves who is boss, second boss, third boss... or bottom of the heap. The hens at the top of the pecking order get the first choice of roost, nesting spot and food. It's not always the biggest chicken at the top; she might just be the canniest.

LEARN TO SPEAK CHICKENISH

If you're lucky enough to have pet chickens, or there are some living in a park near you, you can learn what they're saying.

Dook dook dook! Dook dook! Dook!
COME HERE, I FOUND SOME FOOD!

KUH KUH KUH KA-AAH! KUH KUH KUH KA-AAH!
LOOK OUT!

Brrrrrrrr..... Brrrrrrrr......
I'M BORED.

Ba GAWK! Ba GAWK!
I LAID AN EGG!

BROK-OK-OK BROK?*
IS THAT A BANANA MUFFIN?

* THIS ONE IS UNVERIFIED

HOW TO PICK UP A CHICKEN

1. First, earn the chicken's trust.

Put wheat or fat caterpillars in your hand and hold it flat.

Make soft clucking noises.

2. When the chicken is within reach, confidently but calmly put your hands over her back like this...

3. Hold her wings firmly against her body so she doesn't flap and get injured.

4. Press her comfortably next to your body like so...

5. Tell her all your secrets.

UNDER-REPRESENTED BIRD'S-EYE-VIEWS

A PERSON PEERING INTO A HEDGE

PERCHING IN A TREE FULL OF BLOSSOMS

TWO SECONDS BEFORE SWALLOWING A FISH

HATCHING

All birds in the parrot order have hooked beaks and zygodactyl feet, so they're easy to identify. Apart from that, ANYTHING goes.

SCARLET MACAW
Ara macao

It's very handy to have such hand-y feet

What we usually think of as the most parroty of parrots are the big Amazonian macaws with extra-long tails.

Parrots use their feet to hold their food while they eat it.

The Antipodes Islands are so remote and windswept that no trees grow there. Two different types of parakeets live cheerfully amongst the penguins.

ANTIPODES PARAKEET
Cyanoramphus unicolor

Well, where else am I going to perch?

KEA
Nestor notabilis

This mountain parrot gambols in the snow and will snaffle things from people's backpacks when they're not looking.

Suburban cockatoos rifle through rubbish bins just for fun.

SULPHUR-CRESTED COCKATOO
Cacatua galerita

WHAT ON EARTH.

← Most parrots nest in holes
BUFF-FACED PYGMY-PARROT
Micropsitta pusio
This teeny weeny parrot is about half the size of a sparrow. It eats lichen and fungus off trees, which is very unusual.
BUDGERIGAR
Melopsittacus undulatus
This is what a wild budgie looks like. Sometimes they gather in flocks of 50,000 birds.
VERNAL HANGING-PARROT
Loriculus vernalis
These little green parrots dangle from branches to make themselves look like leaves. They're the only birds known to sleep upside down!
Sometimes called a Dracula parrot because of its vampiric plumage
I vont to suck your... figs and papaya.
PESQUET'S PARROT
Psittrichas fulgidus
Has a bald head like a vulture, but it's for neatly eating fruit, not blood and guts.
Probably the pinnacle of peculiar parrotry
Can't fly
Even though they weigh as much as a pumpkin, kākāpō use their beak and feet like an ice axe and crampons to climb into the tree tops.
Creeps around the forest floor under cover of darkness
Usually alone
KĀKĀPŌ
Strigops habroptilus

OWLS

Owls are irresistibly charming birds, with their wide eyes and saucer faces. And compared to other birds, they have quite a lot of facial expressions.

Although most of the 200 different types of owl are nocturnal, not all of them are.

BURROWING OWL
Athene cunicularia
Hunts during the day and lives in a hole in the ground

Very leggy

NORTHERN PYGMY-OWL
Glaucidium gnoma
Hunts for little birds and mammals in the sunshine

FRONT

BACK

Because owls are always watching you, it's very difficult to see the back of their head.

Maybe I have eyes there too...

Owls can turn their heads so far around it looks like they could go all the way and unscrew like a bottle cap. Fortunately their heads only rotate three-quarters of a full circle, so we don't have a headless owl problem.

GREAT GREY OWL
Strix nebulosa

Owl chicks are called owlets. They take a little while to grow into their faces.

OWL AT SUNSET

I'm thinking about rabbits.

EAR TUFTS →

Some owls have tufty bits that look like ears but they're just feathers. They are kind of like eyebrows, going up or down depending on what the owl is thinking.

LONG-EARED OWL
Asio otus

Stealth mode
Even huge owls can fly in almost perfect silence. Most birds make a swooping sound as the air rushes over their wings, but an owl's wing feathers have a comblike edge to break up the air and stop it whooshing.
Facial disc
Owls use their big satellite dish faces to help them listen. Sound vibrations bounce off the disc and are directed towards the owl's ears.
Enormous eyes
Really big eyes are better for seeing at night because they absorb more light. It's like how the pupil of your eye grows large when you're in the dark and then shrinks when you turn on a light.
Lopsided ears
An owl knows exactly where a mouse is hiding by whether the tiny rustling noise was heard by its left or right ear first. Even more remarkably, owls have wonky ears. One is higher than the other on its head, so the owl knows if a sound is coming from high up or low down.
Feathered leggings
Knifey talons
Zygodactyl feet
Tyto alba
BARN OWL

BIRDS OF PREY

PEREGRINE FALCON
Falco peregrinus

The fastest animal in the whole world

Birds of prey, also known as raptors, include all the carnivorous birds like hawks, eagles, falcons, owls and vultures.

TURKEY VULTURE
Cathartes aura

Naked head so messily eating blood doesn't make its feathers gross.

Vultures have REALLY strong stomach acid that kills bacteria, so eating rotten meat doesn't make them sick.

The sandwich that's been in the bottom of your school bag for 3 weeks can't hurt me.

One of the most likely places you'll spot a bird of prey is on the side of the road between towns. Possums, hedgehogs and other small mammals get squashed by cars, and carrion-eating birds come along to clean them up. They need to keep their wits about them to make sure they don't become roadkill themselves.

Mynas and starlings (which are not raptors) can often be seen bopping along precariously close to speeding cars too. They're after roadkill as well. Very small roadkill. All sorts of insects get splatted by traffic, and mynas are happy to peck up the pieces.

Birds that eat carrion (animals that were already dead when they found them) aren't usually thought of as pretty or friendly. But they're just cleaning up the smelly scraps so you don't have to. Extremely considerate of them.

In fact, many birds snap up free meat if it's available. Flies and their maggots provide a good feast for small birds too. It's easy to forget how important death is to life. We couldn't live without it!

Falcons can catch little birds while they're both on the wing—an incredible skill. Parents train their fledglings to do this by catching prey, flying up into the sky with it in their claws and then dropping it from a great height. The young falcons swoop down to catch it as it falls.

Being a carnivore isn't just about eating other vertebrates. This kite is a bird of prey that hunts almost exclusively for water snails. No high-speed chases here.

SNAIL KITE
Rostrhamus sociabilis

It can be hard to tell exactly what kind of bird you're looking at when it's high above you. Its silhouette will give you a clue though. And it's likely a bird of prey if it's calmly gliding in circles while it searches for prey on the ground.

Birds that are used to being prey are very conscious of anything flying overhead. They look up when a plane flies over, in case it's a raptor.

FLIGHTLESS BIRDS

It seems a shame to go to all the effort of being a bird and then not be able to fly. But looking at it more cheerfully, the reason that some birds ended up flightless is because they enjoyed a life of luxury and ease with almost no predators around to gobble them up. Flying is a waste of energy if you don't have a good reason for it.

If you're going to be flightless, it does help to be very large, very fast or very grumpy. This is the approach that big feathery stompers like ostriches, emus, cassowaries and rheas take.

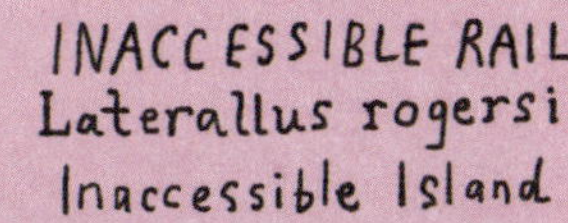

INVISIBLE RAIL
Gallirallus wallacii
Halmahera Island

Remote islands often have their very own flightless birds because when these islands were formed (millions of years ago) birds were able to fly there but their predators couldn't. Being happily isolated like this meant they were perfectly safe living on the ground, where they could eat things that mammals usually had dibs on. This is how New Zealand ended up with so many well-grounded birds, because the only native mammals are bats and sea creatures.

(It's actually just exceptionally shy)

The biggest species of kiwi is only about as big as a goose, but it lays an unbelievably enormous egg. You DEFINITELY couldn't fly if you had to heft that weight around.

THE LITTLEST BIRD

The smallest bird on the planet, the bee hummingbird, is so impressively tiny, it's almost hard to imagine. Fortunately you don't have to imagine because here is a picture of one at full size. You could obscure it entirely from this page with a small carrot or a chocolate bar.

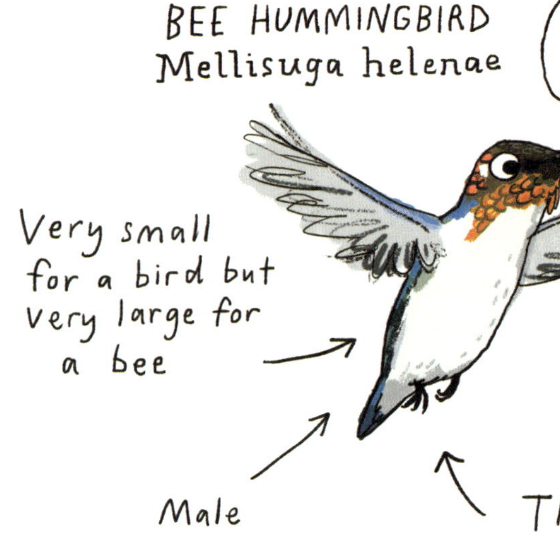

The bee hummingbird's nests are so small, they could build one in an egg cup. Their eggs are only the size of peas.

THE MOST GI

The common ostrich is the biggest bird in the world. It does NOT fit on this page. It would have to crouch down to get on a school bus.

They get their species name, *camelus*, because of the things they have in common with camels. They're both xerocoles (there's a great word for you)—animals with bodies perfectly adapted for living in the desert.

Most unusually, ostriches have just two toes on each foot, making them look almost like hooves. You might wish you had a pair yourself. Ostriches can gallop along at twice the speed of the world's fastest human runners.

THE LESSER SPOTTED

There are more than 10,000 different species of bird out there, and you could spend your whole life being surprised by how they look and what they do. Here are some birds you're less likely to see in your birdbath.

OCELLATED TURKEY
Meleagris ocellata

Like a common turkey, but rainbow!

Bullies other seabirds into regurgitating their food in mid-air and then swoops in to catch it.

ARCTIC SKUA
Stercorarius parasiticus

PURPLE STARLING
Lamprotornis purpureus

A close relative of the common starling, it's got the same body shape but plumage like disco sequins.

WHITE-NECKED ROCKFOWL
Picathartes gymnocephalus

Totally bald face, looks like it's wearing a mask to a masquerade ball

Uncannily smooth feathers that look almost artificial

"Lesser spotted" sounds like a name for an animal that's rarely seen, but it's just describing something small and spotty.

Just to be sensible, here is an actual small and spotty bird.

LESSER SPOTTED WOODPECKER
Dryobates minor

IF YOU COULD BE ANY BIRD IN THE WORLD...?

A FEW SUGGESTIONS

Mallard duck

Can fly, walk and swim (in fresh water or saltwater).

Choose to live in a town or in the country.

People are always giving you food.

Lots of friends around, but you can always fly away for a bit of peace and quiet.

Barn owl

Move as silently as a shadow, very good for sneaking around.

Can see in the dark, very good for spying.

Hear EVERYTHING, very good for learning secrets.

Next best thing to having eyes in the back of your head.

Wandering albatross

Skim over the top of waves the size of houses, just because you can.

See what the whales really get up to when humans aren't looking.

Lots of international travel.

Black-backed gull

No taste will remain a mystery—you can eat ANYTHING.

Live at the seaside or in the country, whatever you're in the mood for.

Watch the world from up really high, like a little god.

Do splats on mean people.

King penguin

Never get lonely; you live with 100,000 of your closest friends and relations.

A diet of very fresh seafood (no hot chips though, unfortunately).

Can hold your breath for nearly 10 minutes.

Extremely good at diving—good for exploring ancient shipwrecks.

Common starling

Mimic and memorize any tune—probably fantastic at karaoke.

Participate in murmurations; it's nice to feel a part of something bigger than yourself.

Quick and nimble, not a big fan of sitting still.

INDEX

I'd just go straight to page 57 if I were you

Alright, where do I lay my complaints???
On page 53 she called me an elongated duck!

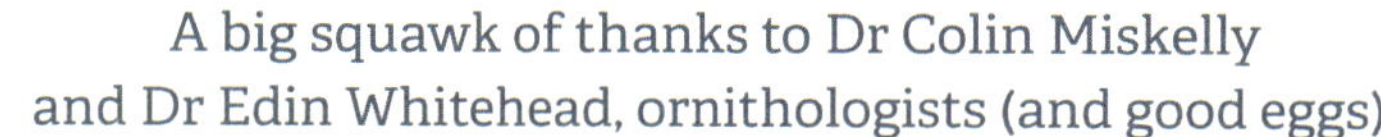
A big squawk of thanks to Dr Colin Miskelly
and Dr Edin Whitehead, ornithologists (and good eggs).

Gecko Press™
An imprint of Lerner Publishing Group, Inc.
241 First Avenue North, Minneapolis, MN 55401 USA

Gecko Press aims to publish with a low environmental impact. Our books are printed using vegetable inks on FSC-certified paper from sustainably managed forests. We produce books of high quality with sewn bindings and beautiful paper—made to be read over and over.

Main body text set in Adelle Regular
Typeface provided by Adobe.

The illustrations in this book were created in Adobe Photoshop.

The author and publisher acknowledge the generous support of Creative New Zealand.

The Cataloging-in-Publication Data for *Omnibird* is on file at the Library of Congress.

ISBN 9798765670514
Ebook available

Designed by Vida Kelly
Manufactured in Nansha, Guangzhou, China, by Everbest Investment Limited,
an accredited ISO 14001 & FSC-certified printer
1-1011635-54075-10/28/2024

For more curiously good books, visit geckopress.com

I don't lay complaints,
only eggs.